Bettie Lake

# Doodling Borders for Wood burning, Gourds, & Drawing

Schiffer Publishing Ltd

4880 Lower Valley Road • Atglen, PA 19310

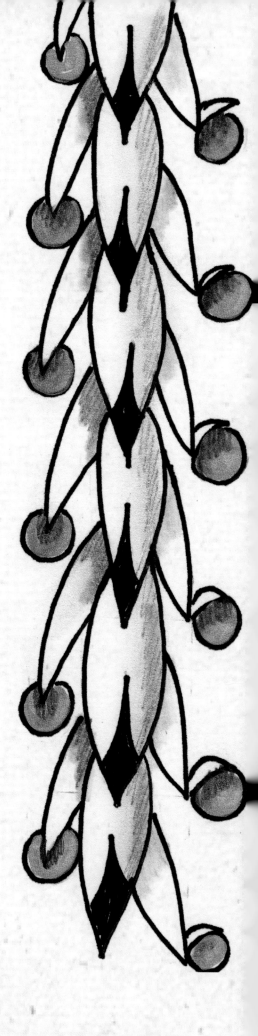

**Other Schiffer Books on Related Subjects:**
*Decorating Gourds: Carving, Burning, Painting,*
978-0-7643-1312-7, $14.99
*Woodburning Basics,* 978-0-7643-2675-2, $14.95

Designed by RoS
Type set in FG Efficient/Tekton

ISBN: 978-0-7643-4750-4
Printed in China

Published by Schiffer Publishing, Ltd.
4880 Lower Valley Road
Atglen, PA 19310
Phone: (610) 593-1777; Fax: (610) 593-2002
E-mail: Info@schifferbooks.com

For our complete selection of fine books on this and related subjects, please visit our website at www.schifferbooks.com. You may also write for a free catalog.

This book may be purchased from the publisher. Please try your bookstore first.

We are always looking for people to write books on new and related subjects. If you have an idea for a book, please contact us at proposals@schifferbooks.com.

Schiffer Publishing's titles are available at special discounts for bulk purchases for sales promotions or premiums. Special editions, including personalized covers, corporate imprints, and excerpts can be created in large quantities for special needs. For more information, contact the publisher.

# Contents

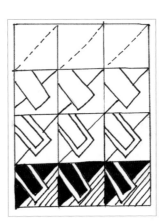

# Introduction

Put a pencil in my hand and I am soon in search of paper. Even as a child, I could be occupied for hours with crayons, coloring books, and plain paper. Doodling is something I have always done! It has helped me focus and calmed me when I've been angry. It also led my great-grandmother to predict that I would grow up to be an artist. She turned out to be right! I spent most of my life drawing and teaching elementary art education. When I retired, I challenged myself to find a new media and ended up with a wood-burner pen and wonderful new friends with an interest in gourd art.

This tool is not an easy one to master and I soon learned that it challenges everyone. Those who can't draw seem to be really frustrated. I see many gourd and wood pieces with images copied from the Internet that are traced onto the surface of soft woods and hard gourds and then wood-burned. The big problem with this process is you can't enter these pieces in competitions, no matter how proficient you become with the pen. Most are copyrighted, a factor that seems to be limiting many wood burners.

I began my gourd art by just drawing my images directly onto the gourd. I went through the process of burning animals, flowers, insects, and other things on wood and gourds, but always found someone who was better at it than I was. I felt defeated before I had even started! I was told I needed patience; my burning skills would eventually meet my drawing skills. I was too impatient for that answer. I was looking for instant success with something unique and different!

I pulled out some of my sketchbooks of abstract drawings that I had been doing for years and realized that the doodling patterns in my sketches might look good on a gourd or on wood, so I created my first doodling border on a gourd and took it to a show. There, someone said that it looked something like a zentangle. Unbeknownst to me, a new art form was moving across the Internet based on my doodling idea of twenty years ago.

I spent the summer researching zentangles and learned to draw several of the patterns on paper, but found many could not be easily wood-burned, so I kept trying different patterns and showed them to my gourd artist friends. As I created more gourds with doodling borders, I found that other gourd artists wanted me to do demonstrations on how I add my doodling borders onto gourds. Suddenly, I am a "hot" new artist with a new process! My doodling drawing classes filled up and the students learning to wood burn were excited to transfer their knowledge to wood and gourds. However, they had the same problem I was experiencing — it was not easy for the beginners.

I had to solve this problem and find a way to move the doodling success from the pencil to the wood burning pen. My solution was to create a set of doodling patterns that build on a simple grid of a square or triangle and to limit the number of lines in each square, doing my best to avoid circles. With my doodling patterns, artists can practice their burning skills and create original art that can compete with any other artwork. The process is as easy as a simple doodle of straight and curved lines.

This book is written for three different kinds of beginning artists: the doodling artists looking for new patterns, gourd artists looking for designs easy to wood burn, and pyrography artists and woodcarvers looking for some new patterns to work with on wood. I teach classes in doodling drawing that I call "zen drawing," as well as gourd art and woodworking demonstrations. All the classes begin with the drawing of these patterns and showing my students special techniques that give their work depth and interest. I then introduce them to the possibilities of the doodling patterns using a wood burning tool. With wood or gourds, the artist has endless directions to take these patterns. After all, patterns are part of every art form.

If you like to doodle or are a fan of zentangles, then I have a section that guides you through my process of drawing, with many suggestions and techniques to turn your doodling into great abstract compositions suitable for framing. I found it easier to practice my burning skills on soft wood before moving to gourds, so my wood burning mentor, Janet Bolyard, has helped me write a section for beginners on how to choose soft woods and pen tips, as well as offering several easy techniques that will help you improve your wood burning skills on soft woods.

In another section, I discuss the world of gourd art for the beginning gourd artist. I talk about where to buy the gourds, how to clean them, and the tools you will need to purchase, along with your wood-burner, to get you started in this art medium. I will also show you some of the tricks and techniques I have learned from other gourd artists, so I hope both the experienced artists and the doodlers will find this book useful. Once you learn the patterns, they allow you to move your doodling skills into any media. Some of the examples I provide come from artists in the areas of ceramics and silk dyeing.

I have improved my wood-burning skills, but I have not mastered this tool quite yet, so I have asked other gourd artist friends to create gourds using my patterns so you can see the varied possibilities depending on the artist's skill. This book is about getting you started with a wood-burner tool and with gourds and hopefully increase your interest in drawing in general. Most of all, it is about having fun doodling and not worrying about getting it to look realistic. There are more than 25 patterns here you can make your own. Feel free to decorate your work with something that is original to you. Just read on and I will show you how!

# Chapter One:
## Learning to Draw Doodling Patterns

All of my patterns are drawn on a square grid or a grid of triangles. Each square or triangle is filled with one to three lines or simple shapes. Nothing could be easier! The challenge is making sure every line connects correctly and the joy is seeing the magic happen when they do!

Doodling Borders in "Zentangle" format

When I am working on good paper, I draw the image and then outline with a black marker. I do just fine with an ultra-fine Sharpie® or you can use a Black Sakura® Pigma® micron 01 pen. I use a white marker as an eraser and recommend a White Sakura GellyRoll®. I also like to carry a small circle guide. For color, I have used colored pencils, watercolor pencils, and Sharpie markers, but I must confess I love to use the metallic colors — especially the gold and silver.

Once I learn a pattern, I create an index card with step-by-step directions and a finished example. I attach these with a ring or I put them in an index card case. This way, they are all there when I need them for a reminder. The card case, my pencil pouch, and a sketchpad are all I need to do my zen drawings anywhere!

Once you have gathered your materials and created your grid card, you can start with any pattern in this book. You will notice that some are more difficult than others, but they are all easy to learn. Take a few minutes to look at my drawings of the patterns in Chapter Two and examine how they are composed and shaded. If you look closely, much of the written instructions I give you will become clearer. Use these as your study sheets! Hopefully they can help you extend your doodling into real abstract art compositions that will impress your friends and encourage you to do more drawing.

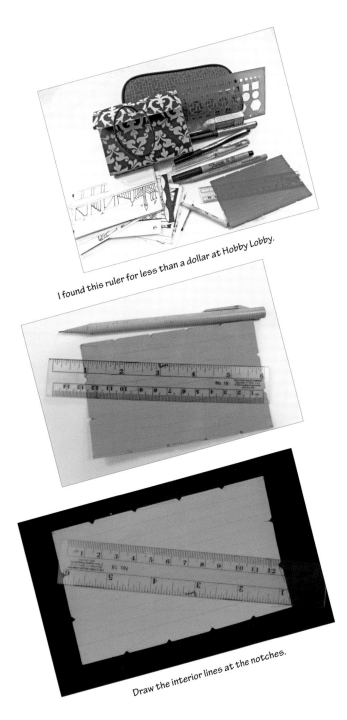

I found this ruler for less than a dollar at Hobby Lobby.

Draw the interior lines at the notches.

To practice the patterns, I use a sketchpad or just printer paper. I also like a soft pencil and eraser. I use a soft mechanical pencil because I don't like to take time sharpening. My favorite tool is a clear plastic six-inch ruler. This one is from The C-Thru Company®. I like it because it is lightweight and will bend on the curve of the gourd! All of my patterns are created with a grid, so I have taken an index card and created a square grid with nine 1" squares. I then notched the points where the lines reach the end of the card. When the pattern has a square grid, I just trace around the index card and use the ruler to create the lines. I also cut an index card in a 1" strip. The stencil used for the patterns with triangles are also drawn within a 1" line guide.

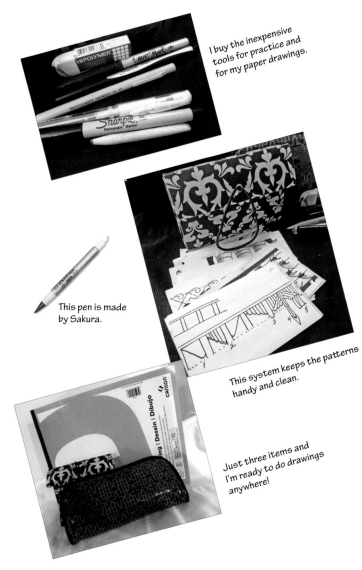

I buy the inexpensive tools for practice and for my paper drawings.

This pen is made by Sakura.

This system keeps the patterns handy and clean.

Just three items and I'm ready to do drawings anywhere!

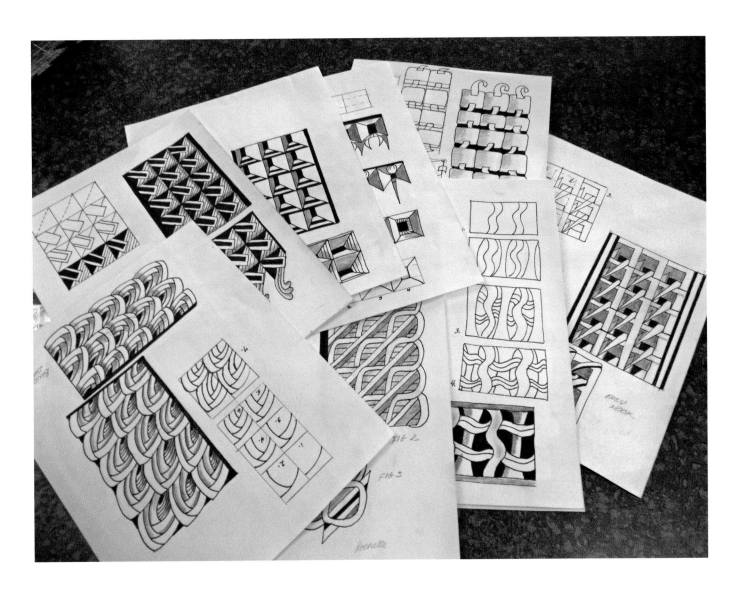

# Chapter 2:
## The Patterns

The patterns are not in any order, so you can start with a favorite or start with one that looks easy. Some are related to each other and I have noted that in my introduction to each. On one side of the page, you will find the directions. You may copy them for your use only! However, I really prefer that you learn to draw them and not rely on any tracing method! On the opposite page, you will find my comments and pictures of the pattern used on different media. I put out a call to many artist friends to help me show you that each pattern is changed by the style of artist, the color used, and the materials used.

This helps me illustrate my point that these patterns should be considered "recipes." You are expected to change them to make them your own. Copyright laws say that if you change the design by 10%–15%, then you are safe — so you can use your variation of my patterns on your artwork and enter it in competition without fear of a lawsuit.

I also encourage you to visit the websites of the artists that contributed to these pages. You will find their website addresses on the last page of the book. And if you do use my patterns for competition artwork, I would love to see it! Please send me a picture!

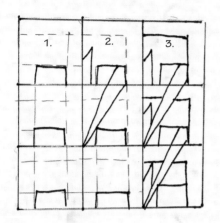

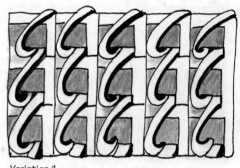

Variation 1

# Easy Hook

When my friend Danielle worked with the pattern, she made the inside square smaller and changed the location of the pointed rectangle. She also made her gourd border swoop downward from the top edge, which I thought was a very creative touch. On the gourd shard, she tried the pattern in a different color scheme. This is a good suggestion to try out ideas on a shard before committing to a gourd. You can recognize my pattern, but it has been altered enough to make it her own.

Gourd shard with pattern example.

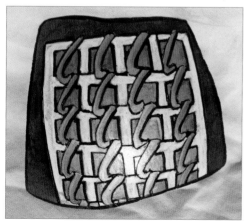

Gourd shard with pattern variation.

Gourd vessel created by Danielle Selby; it's 9" tall and 8" in diameter.

Danielle's shard. Notice the changes she made in color and design.

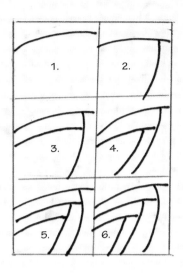
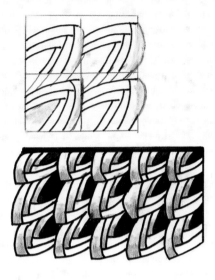

# Band Shell

Once you have created the grid, create a box in the lower left side of the square. Now, add a rectangle on the lower right corner (refer to Step 1). These guide lines are in red so you will know to draw them lightly because they may need to be erased when you finish. Next, you will add the right-pointed standing rectangle. Notice that it goes higher than the other rectangle. Now make the long triangle extruding from the right side of the small rectangle and extend it down the square below, stopping in the lower left corner (refer to Step 2). Darken in the red lines to create the inverted L-shape on the left side of the square (refer to Step 3). For a variation, I changed the elongated triangle to a hook.

Gourd shard with pattern example.

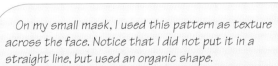

On my small mask, I used this pattern as texture across the face. Notice that I did not put it in a straight line, but used an organic shape.

Mask created by the author; it measures 4" wide and 7" tall.

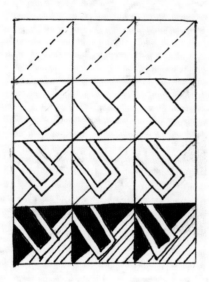
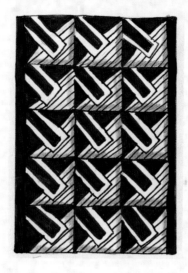
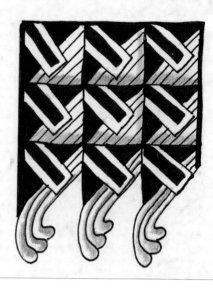

# Acoma

I adopted this pattern from a piece of Acoma pottery. I started collecting this Native American tribe's work when I discovered they used a thin fiber of a yucca plant to paint the thin lines. I really appreciated that skill when I attempted burning lines as close together as theirs! Most of their work is done in black and white with a little terra-cotta, so I have a difficult time imagining this pattern in a different range of colors. I look forward to seeing what my readers can imagine for this pattern.

To practice this pattern, trace your index card grid and complete the interior lines of the grid with your ruler. All of the lines of the square grid are shown, including most of the first diagonal line, which I have drawn as a dotted line — so if you want to trace the grid in ink to practice, you can on this pattern.

Once you have the guide lines in, then draw a rectangle from the top left corner. Overlap the diagonal line enough that the interior rectangle will also cross the diagonal line. Now you are home free! The rest is easy. Complete the inside rectangle and fill the right side of the square with lines — you will determine how many — and the left side of the square with color. Notice that I also added a thick edge down the side. In the variation pattern, I imagined it coming down the center of a piece of art and I ended it with a few easy flourishes.

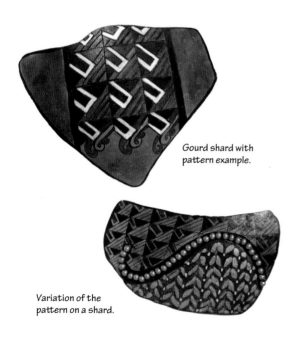

Gourd shard with pattern example.

Variation of the pattern on a shard.

Hellenne did a great job transferring this grid design to silk. The repeated pattern in this square format is very appealing. She tried working with the 1" squares and found it too difficult, so she increased it to 2". This is a good lesson in adapting a pattern to make it work! I really like how she broke up the pattern with the bird in the center. A lovely square scarf! **Silk scarf created by Hellenne Vermillion.**

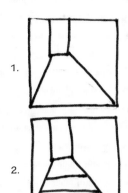

1.

2.

# Dream's Door

This pattern is what my elementary art students used to call 3-D magic art. It was a really big hit in second and third grades, so this should really be easy for any doodlers and even wood burners! This is a square grid with all the lines showing in the final design — so no surprises here. Just an optical illusion!

The magic begins with the door being set off center (see STEP 1). You might want to make a dotted line across the bottom line of the first door you draw and extend it across all the squares so your doors all end at the same spot every time or just eyeball it like I did. Next, connect the corners of the door with the corresponding corner of the square (refer again to STEP 1). Now draw three horizontal lines below the door. Keep them evenly spaced!

The 3-D magic pops when you shade one side of the room's wall and not the other. The door has to be the darkest color you use and the horizontal line just adds interest and more contrast.

Now, look what happens to the illusion when you flip it. At the bottom of the directions, you can see what happens when you change its direction — I seem to be looking into basement windows!

What do you think? Could you put this down the side of a gourd and make it look like holes in the gourd — as if you were looking at its black interior walls?

The pattern is wood-burned on a gourd, and colored with paint and markers.

My dear friend, Gretchen, enjoys creating primitive forms in clay. I like the way she simplified this pattern to fit her style. The pattern was just etched into the surface. No glaze or color was added; instead, she pit-fired the pot to enhance the organic form and style. **Clay pot created by Gretchen Boyer; it's 12" tall and 6" wide.**

11

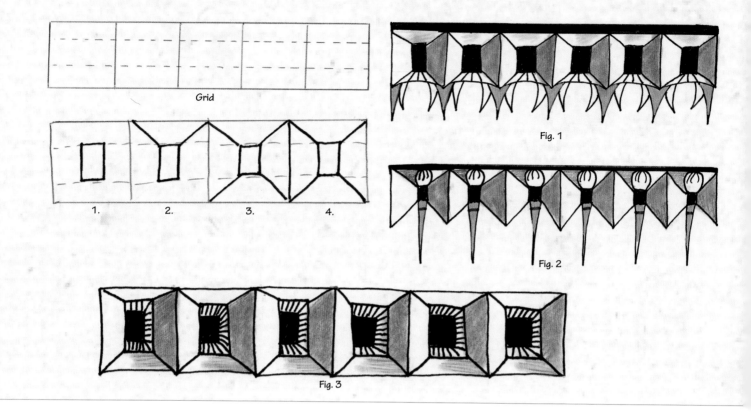

Grid

1.  2.  3.  4.

Fig. 1

Fig. 2

Fig. 3

# Stage Window

This pattern uses only one line of the square grid. A rectangle is drawn in the center within the dotted lines on the grid. This is the stage window! The variation in the pattern depends on the size of the window. In FIGURE 1, the window is in proportion to the rest of the square, but in FIGURE 2, the window is much smaller, and in FIGURE 3, it's larger, with another window inside the first. Also notice that the windows are usually black and only one side of the protruding wall is shaded. This helps create the depth of the box.

On the gourd, I created a wide border of this pattern. This is a great idea if you are a beginner. The larger the pattern, the easier it is to burn and color. The challenge here is the colors you choose. I stayed with colors all in the same family. To add drama, I used a couple of metallic shades of acrylic paint. I highly recommend that you try out your colors on paper first to see which area placement works best for the design effect.

Gourd shard with pattern example.

Gourd vessel created by the author; it is 8" high and 9" in diameter.

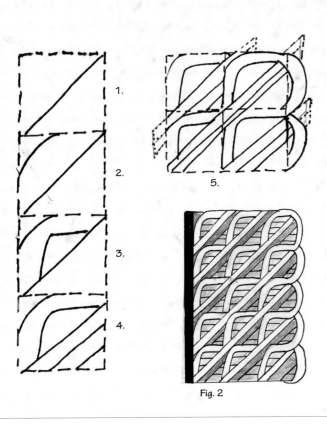

1.

2.

3.

4.

5.

Fig. 2

Fig. 3

# Rochelle

This pattern is a little more complicated than the others done with the square grid. The challenge is getting the double diagonal lines to line up across the pattern, which, in the end, really gives this pattern its character!

Use your index card to create a practice grid in pencil because the grid lines will not show at the end. You also might want to draw them in red pencil or red ink at first until you understand the pattern better.

The first step is to divide the square with a diagonal line. Next, create an arch that cuts off the left corner. Now repeat that curve below the first curve. Imagine you are creating a curving piece of spaghetti! Add two more diagonal lines on the bottom corner of the square and that's it. Just repeat those lines in each square.

Notice how the diagonal line goes behind the bent part of the spaghetti in the finished version in FIGURE 2. The spaghetti also bends at the end of the grid, so you have two options for how you want to have the edge look: confine it to a thick black line or finish the contour line of the spaghetti. Also consider the variation in FIGURE 3 — here, the diagonal ribbon sticks out beyond the bended spaghetti. I also simplified the interior and added the detail to the ribbon line instead of the horizontal line.

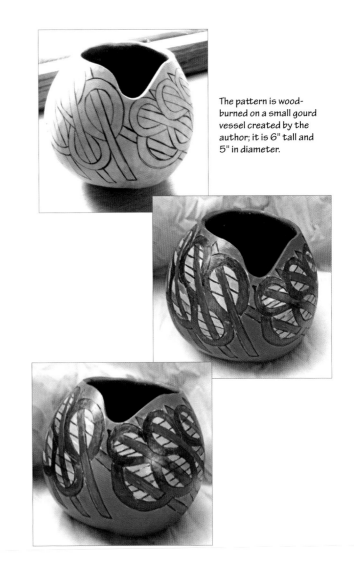

The pattern is wood-burned on a small gourd vessel created by the author; it is 6" tall and 5" in diameter.

13

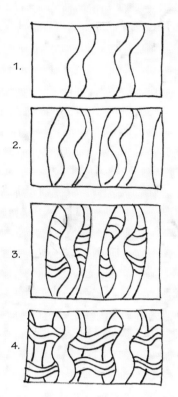

# Flow Weave

This pattern has no grid. You simply have two shapes to alternate, so start with a large rectangle to work within. As in STEPS 1 and 2, alternate curving wide ribbons with tree trunk shapes.

Next, I drew three lines behind the ribbons and in front of the tree trunks. I did this again at the bottom. You could make it more complicated and weave these lines in and out of both of these shapes, but I found that when I added color, the pattern looked too busy. I really preferred this simpler version. Because it is simple, this pattern is good filler pattern. It fills a space, but does not take attention away from the center of focus.

Gourd shard with pattern example.

I used the Flow Weave pattern to cover the surface to help move the eye across the back of this gourd. This was a good choice because the gourd is too small for a pattern more complicated to draw and burn.

Small vessel created by the author; it's 3" tall and 3" in diameter.

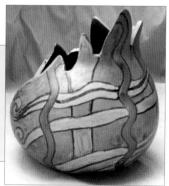

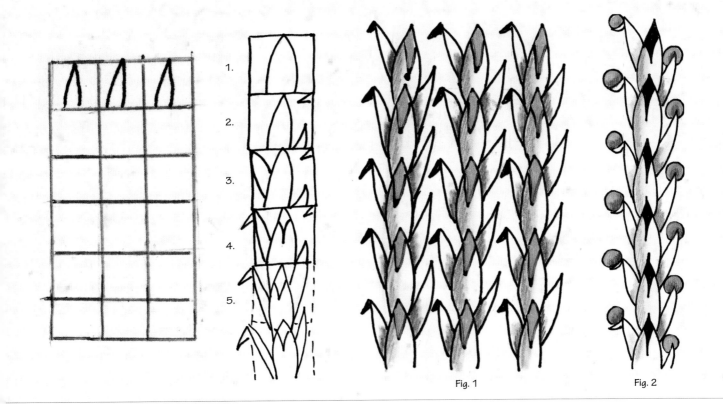

Fig. 1

Fig. 2

# Corn Flower

This pattern is included because we always need some kind of line pattern or filler. This one I created in memory of my childhood in Iowa. I spent many summers watching the corn grow knee-high by the fourth of July. You will need a grid of a single line of squares. It can be straight, but it would be more interesting if it curves. Once the elements are drawn in each square, connect them to each other and then erase the grid.

STEP 1 asks you to draw a shape that looks to me like the top of a lipstick! It must touch both the bottom and the top of the square. In STEP 2, add the tip of a leaf at the top right corner lightly because you might not need this one if you are doing only one line and the tip of a leaf at the bottom right corner. In STEP 3, add another lipstick shape to the center edge of the left side of the first lipstick shape. Last of all, I add the diamond shape to the center (see STEP 4). Now connect all the shapes (see STEP 5) and erase the tip in the upper right if you are not adding another row of flowers as in FIGURE 1.

The variation in FIGURE 2 gives you the option of adding a circle to the tips of the leaves. The depth is achieved by shading the inside edge of the corn husk, near the line where the leaf meets the husk. The black high contrast mark is on the tips of the leaves.

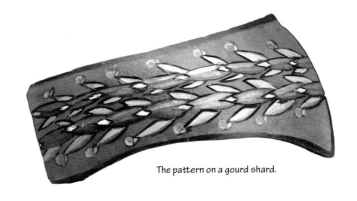

The pattern on a gourd shard.

Since this pattern has a single grid of squares, it was perfect for this small gourd. It is too thin and small for me to wood-burn easily, so I chose to do the pattern in a permanent marker — just simple and sweet. Sometimes you don't need to over-think it!

This gourd, 2" high and 5" in diameter, was created by the author.

15

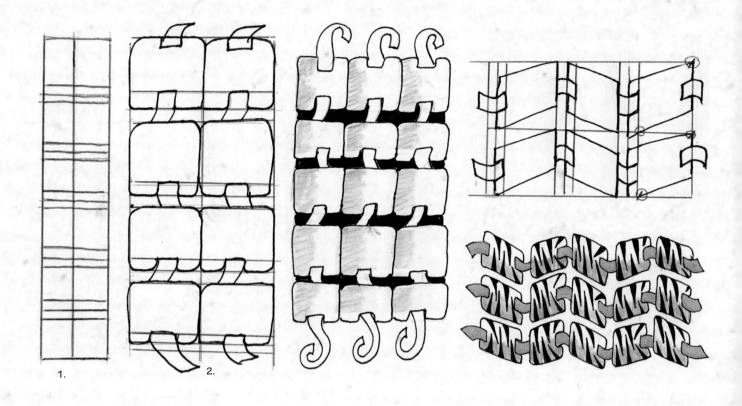

1.   2.

# Tiger Shell

This pattern can been drawn straight or slanted. The lines on the grid near the end of the squares are to help you make sure the ribbon exits the shell at the same spot on every shell and that the space between the shells stays the same. On the second example, you can see that the horizontal lines are slanted to touch the opposite corners of the square.

This pattern has endless possibilities. I've been charmed by the tiger lines and have used both metallic paint on my shard and my gourd example. My friend, Prill, tried using gold leaf with great success, but suggested that the tiger lines would work better if they were not so deep. What other simple shape could go into the shell?

The simple pattern on a shard.

Pattern with tiger stripes on a shard.

Pattern gold leafed by Prill Neagles.

I also used this pattern on this gourd. I combined it with another pattern and kept the design together by using the same color scheme on both. I will talk about this gourd more later on in the book.

**Gourd vessel created by the author.**

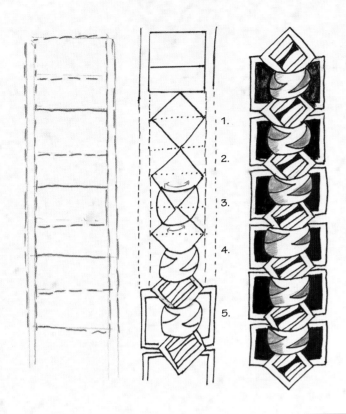

The pattern on a
gourd shard.

# Bowtie

This pattern looks best when drawn large. The grid is a single line of squares with a double edge border that becomes the outside edge of the rectangles that sit behind the bead and diamond chain. Draw this grid in pencil, not ink — you will soon see why! As seen in the red grid pattern, each square is divided in half with a dotted line. This creates the center of the diamond, which is the next thing you draw in every square.

Next, go back and add the beads over the intersection of the diamonds. Make sure you curve the lines in the correct direction (see STEP 3). Erase everything inside the bead and add the details (see STEP 4). Next, add the details in the diamond.

Now look closely at STEP 5 — notice that the background rectangles emerge from either side of the diamond corners. Be careful here: the width of the line you made on the outside line of the grid has to match the width of the line that starts at the diamond. If you are going to change this width, do it now while you are still using a pencil.

In the variation pattern, I eliminated the beads and added the shoe laces coming from the corners of the diamonds. I also discarded the background rectangles and replaced them with two coils that I kept inside the grid space. Just a few changes makes it look very different, so don't be afraid to try out your own ideas!

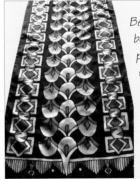

*Beatriz was challenged by the beautiful geometric design of this pattern. If you notice carefully, she included some of my other patterns as well! She said it was very different from her typical colorful, free-flowing designs. How delighted I was when she sent it to me to wear when I talk to others about the book. I love her color choices; it will impress all I meet. It's beautiful! Beatriz's work makes the point that using the patterns in combination will really help make your work stand out!*

**This silk resist scarf, made by Beatriz Castro, is 12" x 36".**

I used this pattern as an emphasis on a gourd that includes many patterns. I intentionally drew it down the center and then surrounded it with another pattern that was more dense and complicated. This helps to make the Bowtie pattern stand out! Left: Pattern wood-burned down the center of the gourd. Right: The pattern colored.

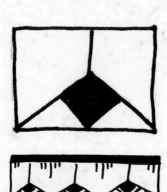

# Dragon's Scale

Here is my revised version of the dragon's scale pattern. It starts with a square grid with the edges of the grid part of your pattern, so you can draw it in ink if you want. Within each square, draw a line halfway down the middle and turn that into the top of an equilateral triangle. Simple and neat!

There are several ways to use this pattern: across the top edge of a gourd vessel, or down the center or sides of a gourd, drawing, or painting. If you're a quilter, you can even edge a quilt with this pattern! Notice how I varied the inner triangle. You could also shade this pattern or use cross-hatching lines.

**Two variations of the pattern on shards.**

On this gourd, I used just two patterns, which curve around the gourd's shape. I put this pattern on vertically and repeated it twice, and then accented it with purple. The curved design creates interest and reflects the sharp edges of the pinecones that embellish the top.

**Gourd created by the author, 5" high and 7" in diameter.**

Gretchen is a multimedia artist who hand-makes paper and also works in clay and interesting yarns. She recently discovered gourds. Here she has created a face on the gourd using this pattern. She then attached it to one of her newly created clay headdress structures and embellished it with yarns and feathers. She was so delighted with the results that she plans to make another one in order to create a pair. It's great to see how artists can adapt gourds to the medium they are already familiar with.

Clay and gourd mask, by Gretchen Boyer, is 6" wide and 20" long.

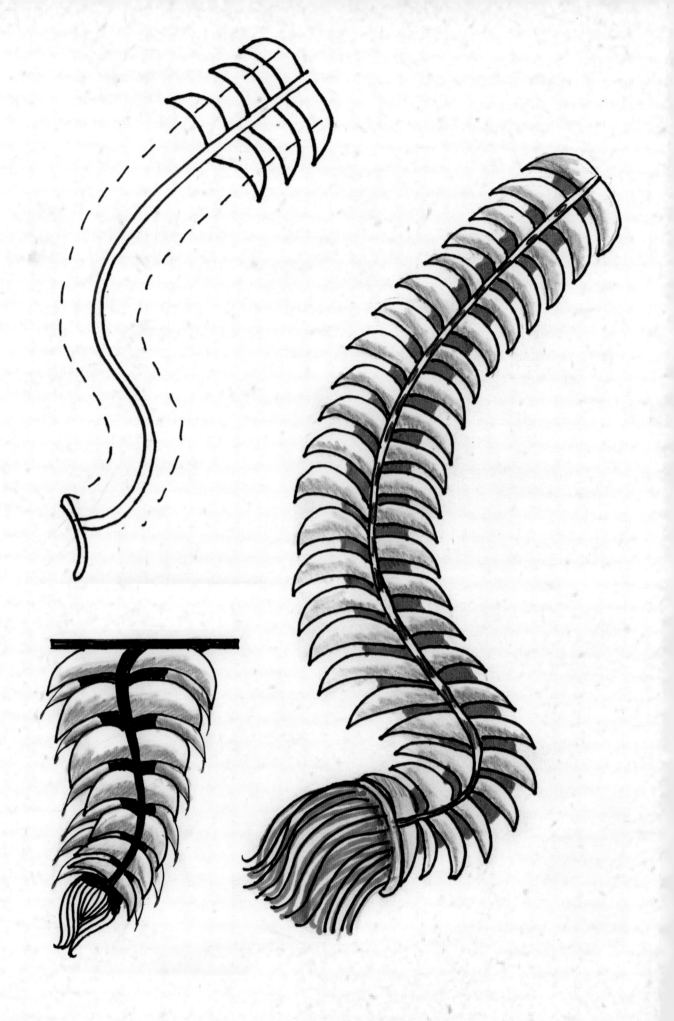

# Dragontail

This pattern was inspired from an idea in a tattoo book. I must admit I have always liked dragons and this experience got away from me. There is no grid here — just a line that waves across the paper, gourd, or piece of wood. Double it to create the spine and add the guide lines to keep the spines even. The space between the dotted lines will eventually be colored in with black or a dark color.

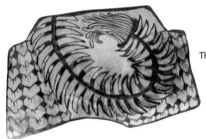

The pattern on a shard.

Dragon Gourd by the author, 8" tall and 9" in diameter.

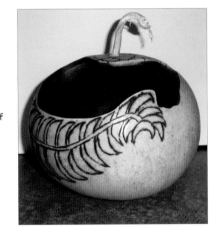

The pattern is wood-burned on the gourd following the curve of the opening.

Large rounded scales cover the back of the gourd.

I must share with you the gourd that was inspired by this pattern. I began by wrapping the tail around the odd opening in this gourd. I left the stem on because I thought it looked like a dragon's head and that inspired me to work with the dragon theme. Next, I created large shapes that reminded me of scales and wood-burned everything quickly, as if I was being timed. I pulled out my copper acrylic paint and covered everything! Still working within the same afternoon, I searched through my embellishments box and found scraps of cactus wood that I turned into wings and a copper scouring pad that I tore apart and wrapped fragments round his neck. I was wild that afternoon — possessed by the gourd fairy and the dragon demon — but the results set my mind on fire for days. Later, I re-thought the scales and came up with a different pattern. I hope this pattern will also set your artistic demons free. Where can you fling a dragon's tail?

# Springfly

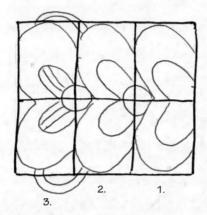

3.        2.        1.

This pattern is on a square grid pattern, but does not reveal the grid in the final presentation. Be sure to practice it on a grid done in ink, so you can erase your mistakes. You will need to practice this one more than once. On your final version, the grid should be marked lightly in pencil. Begin with the thought of a cutout heart. The inside heart begins at the center of the line separating the two squares on the grid. On the pattern illustration I show the outside of heart pressing against the upper edge of the square. If you prefer to complete the curve, then go ahead. Notice I did that on the final drawing when I cleaned it up. I then added a circle. If you are wood burning this pattern and can't do circles, try a rectangle or a triangle.

The pattern on a shard.

Next, I created a narrow ribbon emerging from the top of the circle, then going behind the heart, and then connecting at the center of the next heart. This ribbon goes out beyond the grid. If you want to keep them all at the same point, then draw another vertical guide line beyond each edge of the grid. I did not do that here. I also know some of you want to draw these precisely on your artwork, so I have added some of these extra detail tips.

The variation considers the pattern as a reflection of itself. This might look good down the front or side of a gourd, a clay cylinder, or maybe etched in glass?

Let's talk about creating depth with this pattern. You have many options. By shading the inside edge only, it creates the feeling that the heart curves. The curved lines on the variation pattern also have the same effect. Notice that I made the ribbon line curve from the middle of the circle up and then down to the outside of the heart line. This adds depth to the pattern.

When I finished both patterns, I stood back from it and noticed that I did not have any high contrast. There were no black areas! So I added the black dots in the center of the circles in the original pattern and the black lines in the variation pattern. Remember all of these patterns are always a work in progress and can be changed to fit your purpose.

**Corners must touch**

**7 lines**

# Endless Bloom

This pattern is not really for beginners, although it is not so difficult if you take your time and make sure you get your points attached precisely. The difficulty is in the wood burning. The grid is also different. This time you are working with a square that is divided into rectangles — and none of the grid lines show in the final design! For the pattern to work, the grid must have seven vertical lines in it and the curved lines you draw must touch each other, thus creating an invisible, straight horizontal line.

When I wood-burned the shard example, I did all the curves going in one direction first. I then turned the gourd over and did the curves going the opposite direction. Don't be afraid to do this. Keep turning your gourd, or shard, until you find a comfortable spot. To hold it secure, I sometimes put a bathroom towel under a gourd to hold it steady. Just relax, go slowly, and stop frequently — you do not have to finish the pattern in one sitting.

The pattern on a shard, colored with gold marker.

Silk resist scarf, by Beatriz Castro, is 12" x 36". Once again, we see this pattern in Beatriz's beautiful scarf.

My friend, Bev, collects coyote gourds that grow wild in an area in Prescott, Arizona. They are too thin to wood-burn, so she does a marvelous job drawing designs on them with markers. She then sells them at Christmastime. I was so pleased when she fell in love with this pattern and wanted to use it on an ornament!

Gourd ornament by Beverly Felber. The gourd is 3" in diameter.

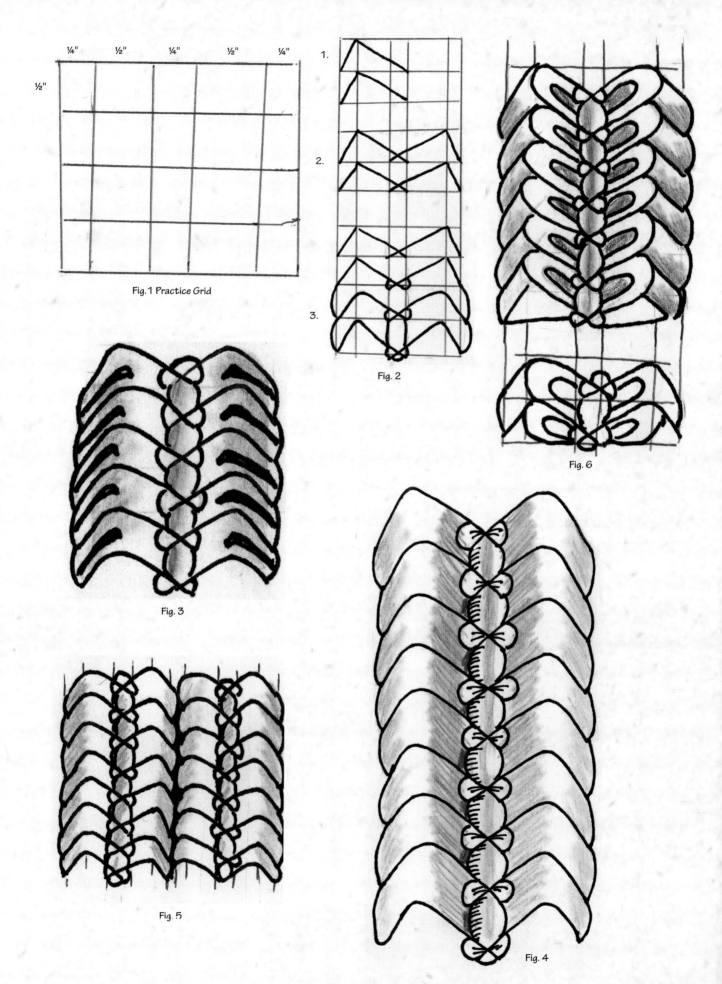

¼" ½" ¼" ½" ¼"

½"

Fig. 1 Practice Grid

1.

2.

3.

Fig. 2

Fig. 3

Fig. 6

Fig. 5

Fig. 4

# Spider Weave

This is said to be the hardest pattern in the book, but I think if you think of spiders in a parade you will be fine! I will admit that the grid is a bit different. The rectangle down the center is half the size of the rectangle on either side of it and the two rectangles on the ends are the same size as the one in the middle. Okay.... so some of you want real numbers to practice with, right?

Make four or more horizontal lines 1/4" apart. They will be 2-1/4"-wide. Now, make your vertical lines at 1/4", then 1/2", then 1/4", then 1/2", then 1/4", as in FIGURE 1 in the illustration.

We are now ready to start making spiders. Each leg fits in the rectangles with the joints touching the corners of the grid as in STEP 1 of FIGURE 2. Fill the entire grid with spider legs on both sides. Be aware that when they get to the middle rectangle they cross each other; at this time, you can turn these into a figure "8" and connect them, as shown in FIGURE 3.

FIGURE 4 is a good way to shade this pattern to make it look like it is a woven pattern. The center pattern could easily change with additional circles or a different kind of knot. In FIGURE 5, I doubled the pattern.

When I wood-burned this shard, I once again burned all the lines going in one direction, turning it so the same stroke motion is repeated. You must make sure the shard is held secure and you are comfortable in your sitting position. Try to stay relaxed and go slowly. Touching all the corners counts on this one!

The last step in the wood-burning process is to add the small hatch lines to help create the shaded effect both on the edge and in the center. You can also leave them out if you prefer.

The pattern on a gourd shard.

Finally, I color it with ultra-fine Sharpies®, so I could blend the colors better. You could also use watercolor pencils. Here, I combined it with some ink dyes. Play around with different mediums on the shards to see what effects you like. You can always trash the shard!

In FIGURE 6, I got a little daring and put a hole in the fold! I kept the hole line parallel with the lines of the fold and then added scalloped lines to the top of the fold and made them parallel to the scalloped lines of the bottom fold. Next, I shaded only one side of the column. I then tried this pattern on a small gourd bowl. The variation is certainly different. I like the three-dimensional effect.

Burn all the lines going one direction.

Notice the cross-hatch lines on the edge of the pattern.

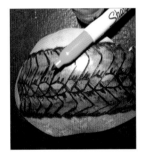

I used markers and alcohol to create the blended shading.

On this gourd, I experimented with the variation pattern. I like it going around the center, but I think it would look better on a larger piece and would be easier to burn! I really enjoy the three-dimensional aspect of the pattern.

This gourd bowl, created by the author, is 5" high and 6" in diameter.

I used the original pattern as part of the headdress on my mask. This piece was too small to burn, so I used markers.

Small gourd mask by the author, measuring 3" wide and 4" tall.

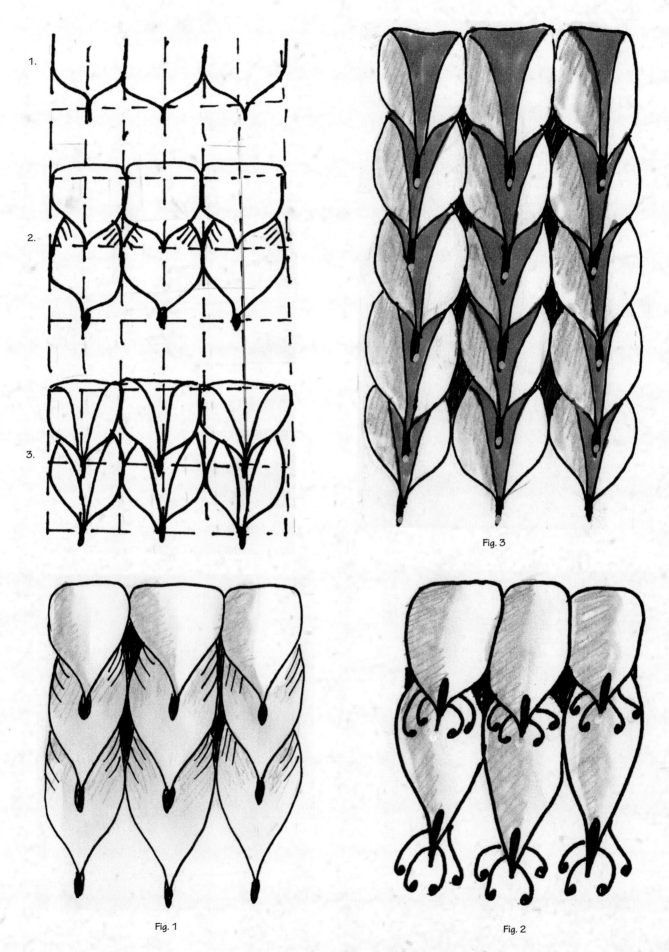

1.

2.

3.

Fig. 3

Fig. 1

Fig. 2

# Cactus Weave

This pattern idea came from my backyard here in Phoenix! I have several agave cacti in my cactus garden. The spikes become like sculptures in the sun as the late afternoon shadows move across their surfaces. You can use the square grid index card for this pattern or simply draw a grid of rectangles.

It does not matter because neither grid will show in the end and the size you choose will decide the length of the spike. If you want long ones, make long rectangles. If you want short ones, make a square grid.

Draw a guideline down the center of each rectangle (see STEP 1) to keep the center point centered. If you have never seen a cactus spike, then think of a teardrop as you practice these.

Curve them at the top (see STEP 2) so they look like they are going under the one above them.

FIGURE 1 is the pattern shaded and then I have drawn two variations to consider. FIGURE 2 shows a more stylized version with a high contrast point colored black between the spikes. In FIGURE 3, the variation is more complicated. I added another line curving down from the top of the spike and meeting at the point, which I then elongated and added a white dot. This new shape has to be a darker color than the spike part underneath it and the tips look best if they're colored black.

I also used this pattern on my mask. The overlapping of the pattern is interesting and almost looks like feathers. It can be used large or small.

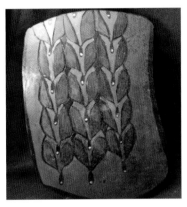
A gourd shard with the pattern.

This gourd mask is 5" x 8"; the pattern is on the forehead.

This gourd is 14" tall and 18" in diameter.

The back side of the gourd with the cactus lace.

Close-up of the fiber on the gourd.

This pattern can also be effective as a dramatic movement across a surface, as shown in this tall gourd. The pattern flows down the side of the gourd, moving the eye away from the interesting edge. The edge of this gourd has cactus fiber sticking out of it. Here in Phoenix, we call it cactus lace. It takes hours to prepare. It begins with a very decayed prickly pear petal. It is soaked for hours until the layers of the skeleton webbing can be separated and cleaned with a tooth brush. You then must lay something heavy on the wet fiber overnight so it dries flat. At that time, you can cut it with scissors to a desired shape. I spray-painted it here with copper paint. On the other side of the gourd, I glued it to a dark surface. You might have to come to Arizona to find it! As it becomes more popular, I bet someone will eventually sell it at gourd shows. Everyone here loves working with the fiber, but chooses to buy it from friends instead of preparing it themselves!

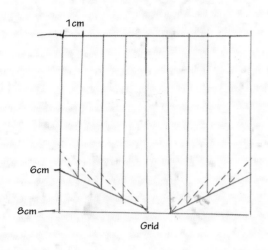

1cm

6cm

8cm

Grid

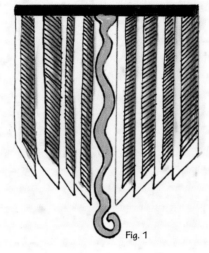

Fig. 1

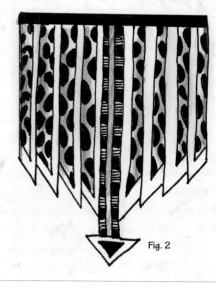

Fig. 2

# Shutter Leaves

This grid is different from all the others. I used the centimeter side of the ruler on this one. I started with two vertical parallel lines, 1 centimeter apart and 8 centimeters long. From the corner, I drew a diagonal line to the 6 centimeter point, and then I lifted the angle of each shutter fold. When I created another rectangle within each fold, it reminded me of French shutters, hence the name, and then when I filled it with dots, it looked like a banner. When it comes to the top and what to put down the center, all your options are open! When I created this gourd, I separated the shapes on the side, but brought them together in the front around a copper embellishment.

The pattern on a gourd shard.

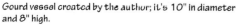

Gourd vessel created by the author; it's 10" in diameter and 8" high.

The back of the gourd.

# Triline

This pattern looks complicated, but when you look at the steps you can see that there are only a few lines within a triangle. The complexity comes when you reverse the triangles in a strip between parallel lines as we have done with many other patterns in this book. If you are a gourd artist, keep this pattern large because it is rather hard to do on a curved surface. On a flat surface where it can be shaded, it is a great deal of fun because the depth-of-field can really be played with through shading and choice of colors. I have shown you two variations. The pattern with the dark triangle has more impact than the second one, which I might prefer as a secondary pattern or a background pattern. You can see that I used it as a secondary pattern on the tiger shell gourd.

It has a very small area at the top with a steep curve. A difficult place to add detail! The curving lines of the pattern move your eye to the embellishments at the top of the gourd, but does not distract from the tiger shell pattern I put across the middle of the gourd. Keeping both patterns in the same color family helped keep the composition consistent throughout the design on the gourd.

I kept the triangles large because they were on the steep curve at the top of the gourd. The lines of the pattern also helped lead the eye to the top of the gourd and the embellishments.

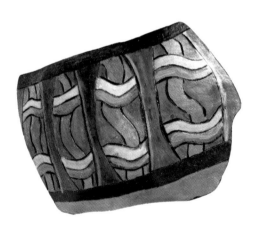

Gourd shard with the pattern.

Small gourd bowl created by the author; it measures 3" high and 3" in diameter.

This is actually the top of a gourd cut off to create an opening on another vessel. The gourd was too thin and too small to wood-burn. I carefully used my gourd saw to re-cut the top: I broke it, but just cut it further and ended up liking the shape. I used this simple pattern going horizontally around the bowl and made the vertical lines come from the peaks on the rim. Everything is in markers; once again, I used my metallic blues. Simple and sweet!

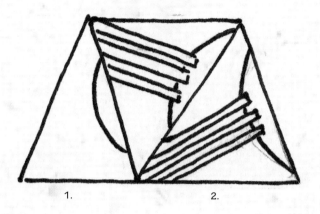

1.　　　　　2.

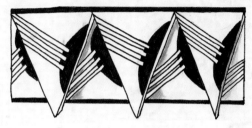

# Pan's Pipes

This pattern is based on a triangle. Draw two parallel lines. Between the lines, draw a zigzag line that creates equilateral triangles where the tips touch the parallel line. The secret to this pattern is to work on one side at a time and then flip the pattern and work on the opposite triangles. Otherwise, you are just going to end up confusing yourself!

To get started, draw half a circle against the right side of the triangle (see STEP 1). Repeat that on all triangles facing you. When you are finished, flip your pattern strip over and draw the half circle on the left side of these triangles. To clarify, look closely at the illustration and notice that the circles are drawn on opposite sides of the triangles on each side.

The pipes, or rectangles, begin from the corner of the triangle and go up the sides. Don't go too far into the circle. You need much of the circle to stay black to keep the high contrast. Also notice that the variation pattern has a perspective edge on it and goes beyond the parallel line. The shading on this inside edge also adds to the illusion that the protruding triangle is thicker.

I have always kept the short diagonal line light while the circle behind them was dark — and I have never used it vertically. You might want to try reversing that, but I just can't get pass the simple beauty of the lines. What a surprise I had when Anna sent me this image of her variation. Maybe you can also venture away from the basic pattern.

The pattern on a gourd shard.

The pattern is wood-burned onto the gourd.

Finished gourd created by the author; it measures 8" tall and 13" in diameter.

I was excited when Anna notified me that she wanted to use this pattern. However, she said she would have to change it to work in clay. I told her that was my intention with the patterns. The medium will always dictate how the pattern will work best — and that is what makes it Anna's original design! This is a great example and I am thrilled to share it with you. **Bas relief wall-hanging with glazes and underglazes. Created by Anna Mayes, it measures 6-1/2" x 11".**

# Bamboo Line

This pattern is a simple line grid of rectangles. There is one cord on the left of the grid line and three on the right. The variation in the pattern comes in the addition of the leaf shape at the bottom and in the color choices you make. Gourd artist, Karen Friend, chose to limit the colors of the chords and she combined the grid lines to create a band round the center of her gourd and eliminated the dangling leaf.

Notice, she also reversed the diagonal pattern across the center. This lovely gourd is a great example of how you can play with my patterns and take them in another direction. I love the idea of putting these shapes together with the bird of paradise flower! She saw something completely differently than I did.

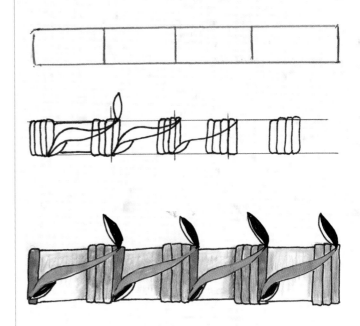

Bird of Paradise Gourd created by Karen S. Friend. It measures 9" wide and 7" tall.

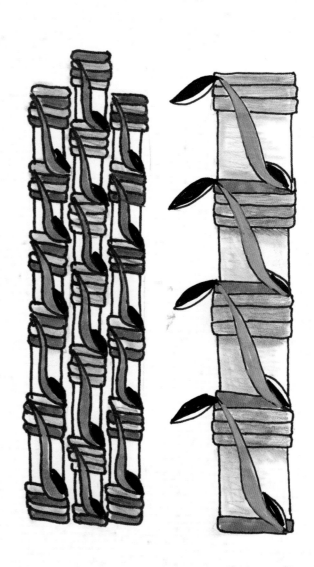

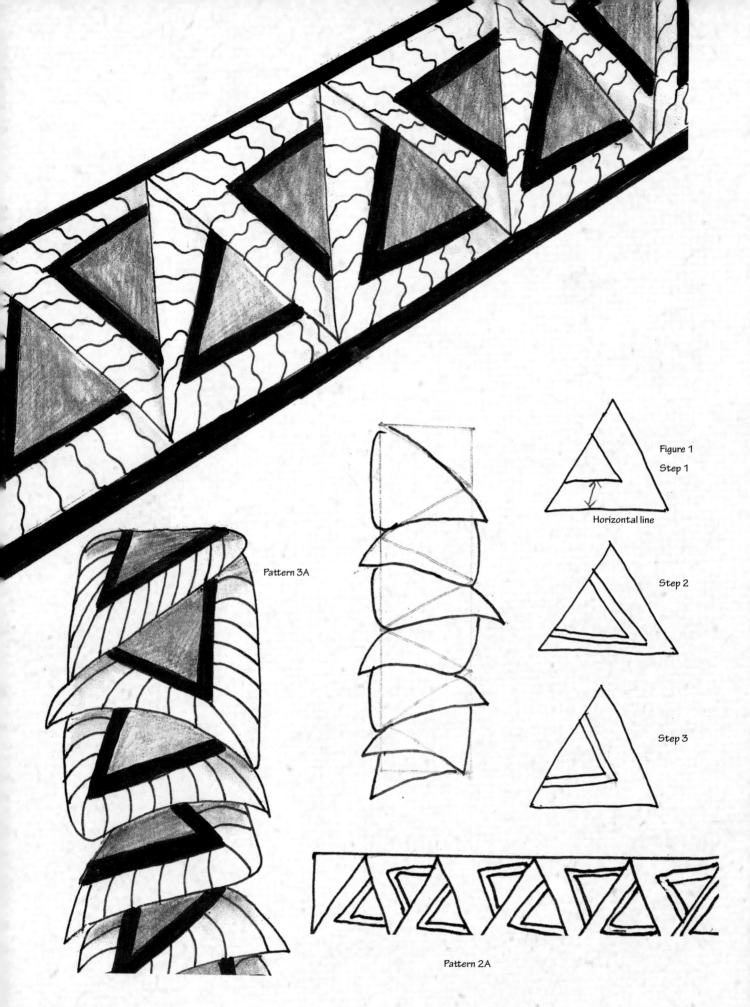

Pattern 3A

Figure 1

Step 1

Horizontal line

Step 2

Step 3

Pattern 2A

# Origami

This pattern is based on a triangle. It can be drawn tightly within two parallel lines or more loosely as overlapping triangles. I want to first cover how to create the triangle on the interior of the large triangle because that will become confusing once you loosen up the outside triangle.

The rule you must remember is that the bottom of the horizontal line of both the inside and outside triangle must stay parallel. Please refer to the illustration (FIGURE 1).

To create pattern 2A, begin with two parallel lines and create a zigzag line of triangles, making sure that the points of the triangles touch the edge of the parallel lines. Draw the interior triangles on one side at a time. Do not work on the triangles upside-down! It never works out right for me.

What kind of line pattern you use on the edge of the big triangle depends on the density you are seeking. Remember: the closer the lines, the denser the look of the overall pattern. If you are wood burning, the wiggly lines may not be a good choice.

To create pattern 3A, I started with a vertical grid of triangles and then stretched out the corners of each triangle beyond the grid edge, creating a curved triangle. I also curved the interior lines to enhance the same feeling.

On both patterns, I wanted the viewer to think that one triangle was coming out from under the one on top of it. To achieve that illusion, I shadowed the corner areas. Study the illustration for a moment to understand this tip.

On this gourd, I used the variation example down the center and wrapped a border around the top. Once again, I kept the patterns large on the gourd. The embellishments also add to the impact of the gourd and are always fun and challenge my creativity. Here, I used a piece of cactus wood, which I painted metallic bronze and then added turkey feathers. **Gourd created by the author, measuring 12" high and 6" in diameter.**

My friend, Dar Saucedo, offered to create a gourd for this book and quickly picked this pattern out. She really made it something dramatic. She sent me two bowls! The small one is decorated on the bottom! She has displayed it wonderfully and I love the way the pattern crosses itself! The other is a large bowl with a simple treatment of the pattern traditionally around the top of the gourd. Two gourds that are real treasures! **Gourd bowls created by Darlene (Dar) Saucedo. Large bowl, 4" tall x 10" wide. Small bowl, 5" tall x 6" wide.**

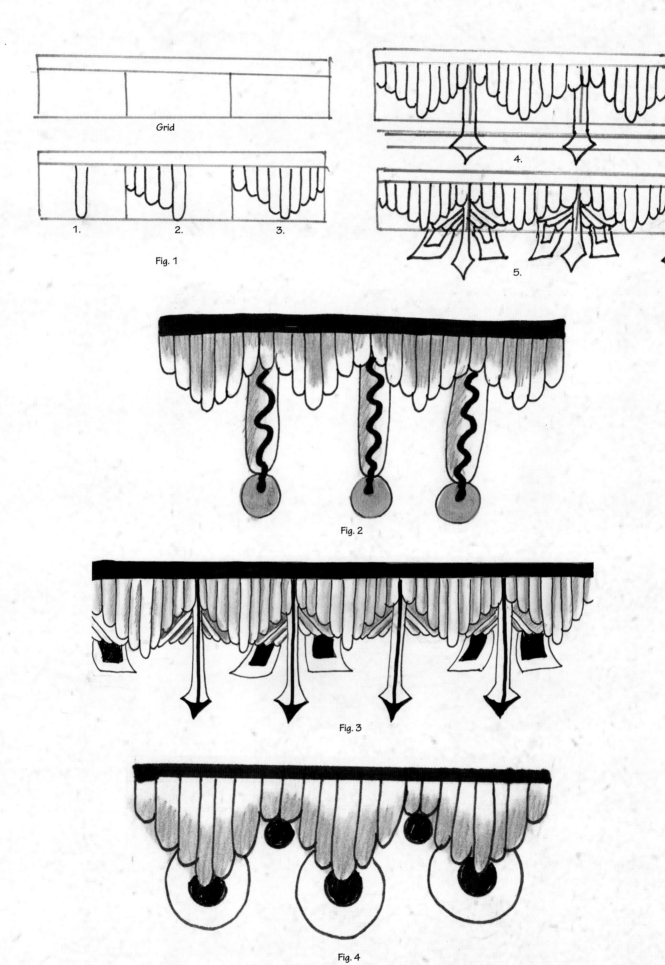

Grid

1.    2.    3.

Fig. 1

4.

5.

Fig. 2

Fig. 3

Fig. 4

34

# Cathedral

This pattern is the basis for Trumpet Weave and Ray's Binding, which are harder, so we are starting with this one first. There are so many directions to take this pattern, I just couldn't stop! I will begin by saying that drawing this pattern is easy, but wood-burning it is not. When I look at this design, I imagine a clay artwork with large coils of clay hanging from a rim of a vessel! Keep this in mind as you draw this pattern. When I wood-burned it (see FIGURE 1), I burned all the lines going one direction, curling the bottom tip slightly, and then I turned the gourd and did the other directional lines, making sure the curled tips touched. Go slowly with this process. It takes practice, but it's a cool stroke to learn!

The grid is a single line of rectangles with a bar across the top. There are three basic steps before the embellishments: Step 1 starts with one of those clay coils down the middle of the rectangle; Step 2 asks you to add four to the left side, making them shorter as you go; and Step 3 asks you to repeat that on the right side.

The next steps set up the guide lines for the pattern in FIGURE 3, which is the most complicated. FIGURES 2 and 4 are simpler, but do include circles. Also, take notice that the shading varies on all of these.

The last thing I would like you to consider is that this pattern turned into a circle. Take a look at illustrations 9 and 3 on pages 42 and 43. Notice how I turned the bar into a circle and built my grid around it.

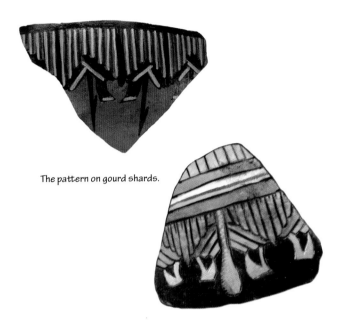

The pattern on gourd shards.

On this gourd, the doodling border fills most of the space and is set off by the black bottom. This design element is now part of my own stylistic approach. The black covers up any dents, bumps, or stains that are often near the bottom of the gourd. I use a high gloss black acrylic paint.
**Gourd bowl by the author, measuring 5" high and 6" in diameter.**

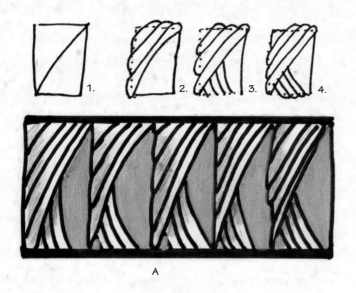

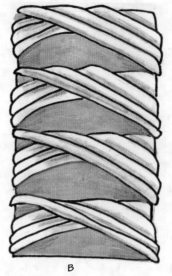

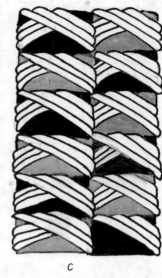

A

B

C

# Ray's Binding

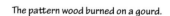
5.

This pattern starts with a row of vertical rectangles, which I want you to make-believe we are going to wrap with big coils of clay that are as thick as a water bottle! Got the picture? Great! Now let's play!

Draw a line diagonally across the rectangle (see FIGURE 1). Complete the line to form a coil shape. Do this two more times. Next, make the coil lines curve to the left on the bottom (see FIGURE 4); notice how I made it bumpy on the bottom of the coils.

See how easy this pattern was.

However, if you are wood-burning, it isn't easy. Think of each coil as two curved lines that meet (see FIGURE 5). Burn all of them going to the right and then turn the gourd, or wood, around and burn all the curves going to the left. Remember to go slowly. This does take practice, but if you master this stroke it shows up again in this book and is very versatile.

In the illustration, I have three variations: PATTERN A is drawn between two parallel lines that don't allow for overhang; PATTERN B shows you how it would look going vertical using large rectangles; and in PATTERN C, I have created two rows of rectangles that are smaller and then I alternated the color in the interior space, which adds to the woven effect.

The pattern wood burned on a gourd.

This pattern was used to wrap around another pattern centered on the gourd. The overall effect has great depth and looks more complicated than it is — that is the beauty of these doodling patterns when used in combinations, and this gourd is a great example. I hope it inspires you to try one.

**Gourd created by the author, measuring 11" tall and 12" in diameter.**

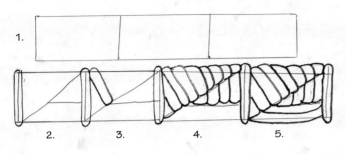

1.

2.    3.    4.    5.

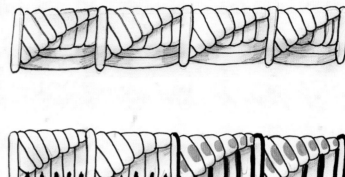

# Trumpet Weave

This pattern is based on a single grid of rectangles and one shape that I like to refer to as a coil. Each rectangle is divided in half with a diagonal line and a horizontal line. Each vertical line of the rectangle is surrounded with a coil. From the right side of the vertical coil, draw one diagonal coil (see FIGURE 3) and complete the double roll (FIGURE 4). Now, add two horizontal coils across the bottom. In the variation pattern, I eliminated the bottom horizontal line and replaced it with vertical coils with high contrast details, plus a little shading.

Another important detail that adds to the depth illusion is the extension of the coil edge over the edge of the rectangle. This scalloped, bulged edge makes the viewer think that they are looking at thick yarn or clay. I also shaded where the two sets of coils overlap.

On my small, round ornament gourd, I drew the pattern large around the center. I then used a dye on the gourd and let it dry overnight before I began the drawing process with the markers.

A standing gourd ornament by the author, measuring 3" in diameter.

# Braid Dance

1.

2.

Fig. 2

3.

Fig. 1

Fig. 3

Fig. 4

We are going to put our coils across triangles going opposite directions. Lightly draw in the zigzag line of your triangles (see STEP 1). As with the other triangle patterns in this book, do all triangles going one direction first and then reverse, or turn the paper, and do all triangles going the opposite direction. Now, wrap three coils diagonally to the left on all the triangles, pointing that way as in FIGURE 2 (see STEP 2). Refer to STEP 3 to see how you will turn the paper around to fill in the remaining triangles with lines going the other direction. FIGURE 3 illustrates the final pattern while Figure 4 shows another way to shade the braid. The secret here is to go slowly and try to keep the coils all the same size.

So…you now think you have this coil thing perfect, right? Well, not so fast. Here's the challenge question: in FIGURE 3, the vertical grid lines show, but they don't show in FIGURE 4 — how did I do that?

This was a rare gourd. A nice shape and stem and a surface I just couldn't paint. To move the eye around the gourd, I curved two patterns. The Braid Dance pattern draws the viewer's attention and the texture is greatly complemented by the Dragon Scales pattern next to it, which reflects the pointedness of the pinecones that embellish the top. If the shape is perfect, the surface flawless with a good stem, and it stands straight and firm, don't walk away from that gourd!

One of the artists I asked to make a gourd for this book was a lady who has won more ribbons than anyone I know. When she said she wanted to do several of my patterns, but much smaller, she asked, "Can I really change them to fit my need?" The answer to her question is the same to all of you who want to consider trying these patterns in your media. By all means change them! Any good recipe provides the essential ingredients to give the dish a successful foundation. This is how I consider my patterns. They are meant to guide and inspire, and this is what Jane has done with her vessel. Her talent for fine detailed wood burning work is awe-inspiring and, at first, I didn't see my patterns, but when I looked closer, the strokes revealed themselves to me and I became intrigued with her variations on my themes. Upon reflection, that is what I hope you take away from this chapter — permission to let your own creativity soar. Change these patterns to make them your own and feel free to enter your work into competitions and galleries. Once again, Jane has challenged my interest in gourd art with her unusual pieces and reminds me my wood burning skills need more practice!

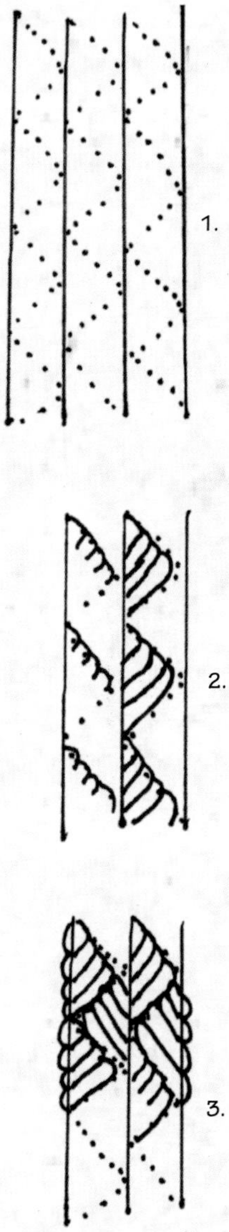

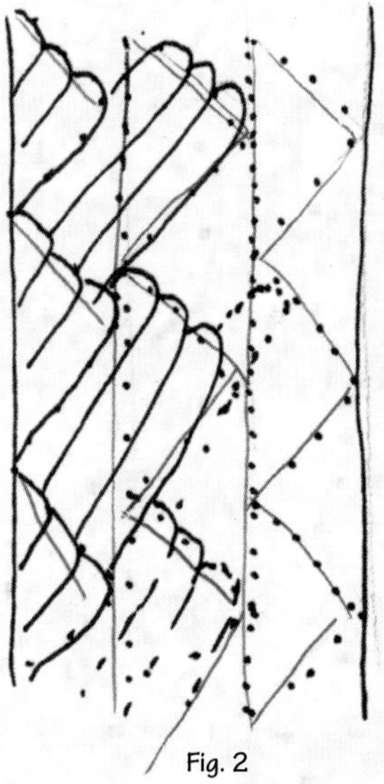

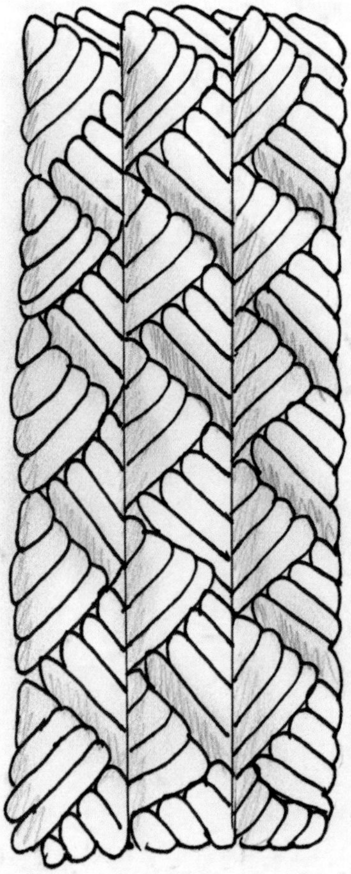

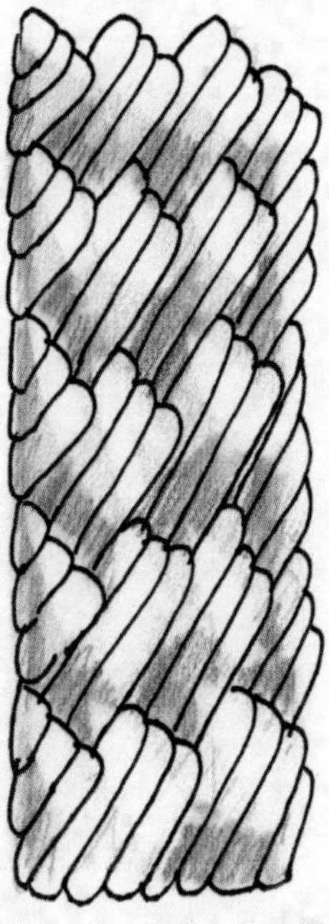

Gourd created by the author,
measuring 6" tall and 8" in diameter.

The pattern on a gourd shard.

Gourd vessel by Jane Boggs, titled
*Contemporary Visual Texture.*
It's 18" high, 8" wide, and 6" deep.

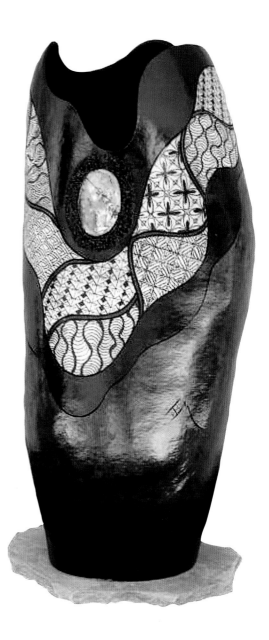

Now that you have seen the patterns and the possibilities, this is what I suggest you do: PRACTICE! Begin on sketch paper, and then move onto good drawing paper. Create your travel pattern cards and apply the patterns to your own medium. In the next sections, I provide more tips on drawing the patterns as elements in an abstract drawing, and then if you are looking for a challenge, pick up a wood-burning pen. Great fun awaits you as you learn how to burn lines into soft wood and gourds. This book is full of tips that can get you started. I will share all I know.

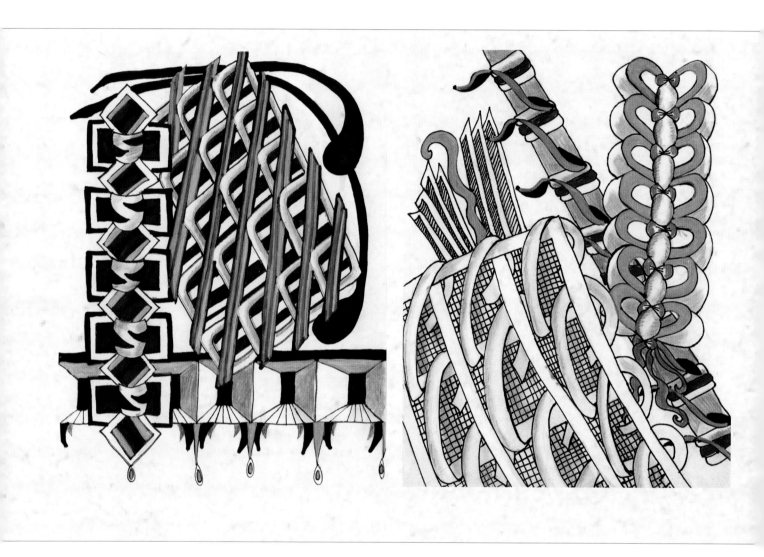

## My Journey from Zentangles to Doodling Borders

Some of you may be aware of a new drawing format called Zentangle®. I first found it on the Internet when a friend mentioned that my work reminded them of zentangling. In the past few years, it has grown into a blog art form. The format was established by Maria Thomas and her husband, Rick Roberts, and you can read about their idea and how it became a business at www.zentangle.com.

Their non-representative drawings, or zentangles, are made up of patterns, or tangles, drawn on a small tile of paper that is to be completed in about fifteen minutes.

A Zentangle tile is 3-1/2" square on heavy white paper. To keep the cost down, I practiced on line-less (3" x 5") index cards that I cut to 3" x 3". The design is drawn with a Black Sakura® Pigma® micron 01 pen. There are no mistakes, so erasers and pencils are not needed. Any mistake can be turned into part of the design. Since the format is so small, you are encouraged to keep turning the paper. These designs are only non-representational, so direction of the elements is not important.

The small format also attracts both non-artists and artists on-the-go. Students are encouraged to enter a state of relaxed focus in which intuitive insights flow freely. You are reminded that there are no mistakes, so non-artists and doodlers are encouraged by this art form and help is available on the Internet. Many gather at Linda Farmers' site, www.TanglePatterns.com. She will e-mail you a new pattern every day and link you to the blog artists who create zentangles and sponsor challenges. It is a great way to make artistic friends all over the world!

My zen drawings really go beyond a zentangle, however. They are done in a 9" x 12" sketchbook with 20-pound paper. This heavy paper discourages the bleeding of the felt tip pens. You can practice on 11-1/2" x 8-1/2" computer printing paper when you are learning a new pattern or a sketchpad with lightweight paper. Buying top quality paper and pens that are made just for this art form is not necessary. That's why I have listed my inexpensive choices in this book for you to consider.

My compositions are both representational and non-representational. I really like the challenge of positive and negative space and the effect the density of a pattern has on the composition so I use color sparingly. I do like hints of metallic color via markers. I enjoy adding shading to my work and focus on getting the right pattern to fit both my composition and my need for density. All of my compositions begin with a light pencil outline. For the abstracts, I make sure my elements overlap each other to add to the illusion of depth, which I later enhance with shading. This is why my patterns look like they are popping off the page.

My zen drawing style is very portable and non-intrusive. I usually do my drawings at my dining room table while listening to a TV program, or I will take it along on a fishing trip with my husband. He fishes while I enjoy the scenery and complete a drawing. This is why I keep my tools and supplies portable. If you would like to see more of my zen drawings, I invite you to visit my Zendrawing Gallery at www.zendrawinggallery.com.

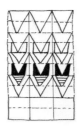  

Illustration 1

Illustration 2

I have enjoyed teaching zen drawing to both children and adults: no one fails with my drawing technique, zendoodling. In fact, most students find it great fun. I am fond of saying that if you like to doodle, then this method — zen drawing — will be easy because I have just put doodling on steroids!

The patterns in this book will provide you with a place to start with this art form. My patterns cannot be found on the Internet, nor are they shared in the blog world. If you consider yourself a zentangle artist, then these patterns are new ones for you to learn. If you would like to learn more about my style of drawing, then focus more time on the drawing chapter and take a closer look at the abstract drawing I included using the doodling patterns.

If you are learning to be a better wood-burner or gourd artist, then be sure to read closely the chapter that introduces you to these two art forms. Notice how my patterns can be easily used with a wood burning tool. I have great fun with my gourds and love sharing my tips and secrets at gourd festivals and patches. I am always amazed at the number of people I meet at woodworking shows who are doing amazing artwork with their wood-burners and different kinds of wood. We all seem to be looking for more ideas and I hope you will consider these patterns for your next project and share them with me via e-mail. I wrote this book just for you.

# Using the Borders in Abstract Drawing

Once you have begun to practice the patterns, you can take a few at a time and begin to create abstract drawings. I usually start my students with three to four patterns in the first drawing and they continue, following the same process to practice the other patterns. By combining them and filling the patterns inside unusual shapes, you will begin to feel comfortable enough to burn them into wood or even apply them on other surfaces — so don't skip over this part, especially if you don't consider yourself a good drawer. It will build your self-confidence and it is very relaxing!

This style of drawing is so relaxing because there is no pressure to make something realistic, just something recognizable. Here, we are only talking about geometric shapes! The secret is in the composition and how you use your pencil to represent light, so we will start with only black and white.

That means you will need only the supplies you used to create the patterns. Gather a soft pencil, your ruler, your grid index card, an eraser, and an ultra-fine line marker. Twenty-pound drawing paper works well; I like the 9" x 12" size.

To illustrate the details of the technique, I will be referring you to the illustrations I have provided for you in this book, so be sure to stop and check these to examine what I am talking about. Remember: the magic is in the details!

As an artist, you have about five seconds to pull the mind's eye in and across your artwork. There is no subject matter in an abstract, so the composition has to do the work. Let's reveal some composition secrets! First, notice how the borders overlap one another. This pulls the composition together and allows your mind's eye to flow from one pattern to another, but also notice that there are empty areas where the eye is allowed to rest. Sometimes I put these between patterns and sometimes around the sides. Do not fill the entire page with patterns! It will only confuse the eye and the mind will refuse to focus! However, I also make sure that some of the patterns go off an edge or two — this allows the mind to imagine what it might be missing and focuses it longer on your images.

To help the mind see depth on the paper's two-dimensional surface, I need to create the illusion that one pattern is lying on top of another. If you want an edge to look like it is coming out from under another, like on the Origami pattern in Illustration 9, then add a shadow where they meet. To do this, I have placed a shadowed area where one border crosses another one. Also, if you want an edge to look round, shade in only the inside edge, like I did on the Band Shell border and the Corn flower in Illustration 5. Another great pattern to do this with is Springfly in Illustration 3. Also notice how I took Cathedral and put it around a circle. Just because you learned it on a straight line doesn't mean it has to stay there!

Illustration 5

Illustration 9

42

Illustration 3

Illustration 12

On many of the patterns, I have suggested variations and then I purposely changed where I put the shading. The true rule for shading depends on your light source direction. The farther from the light, the darker the shadow or shading. You are the artists: experiment! Try shading your patterns in different ways until you find what you like. The last trick to reveal is the use of two tools. The artist stump is used to blend the soft pencil, which I usually color in at an angle as evenly as I can. By the way, this tool replaces your smudging finger. The other tool is the soft eraser. If you erase the area right next to the darkest area you shaded in, when you finish it, you will have created extra contrast — I always do this on the opposite side of each blade of the Dragon's Tail.

Abstract drawing with pencil can be very rewarding. Once my young art students understood shadows and the shading techniques, their drawings looked more three-dimensional (or 3-D, as they told their friends proudly). It takes only a few tools and you are on the trail to drawing more realistic objects. Once you feel more confident, try this experiment. Sit in front of a simple object (coffee cup or apple) and squint your eyes. Continue this until you begin to see the contrast between the shadow areas and the light areas. Now…try drawing it and adding the shadows. You are now on your way from a doodler to an artist!

What if you are sitting somewhere with only a pen and paper? You can still shadow and shade using dots and lines. In the art world, it is called stippling and cross-hatching. "Google it" on the Internet under images and you will see how easily it works: the closer the lines or dots, the darker the shade or shadow. I used stippling and cross-hatching on Illustration 5.

The patterns that involve an optical illusion also work well in an abstract drawing. In Illustration 12, I played around with Stage Window, Dream's Door, and Shutter Leaves. What works well here is the overlapping of the images and the one diagonal element that adds the drama. The other drama element is the circle pattern in the Shutter Leaves pattern.

These are known by many names, but they are useful for shading and a must-have for these patterns.

Sometimes, when I am creating my zen drawings, I begin with organic shapes and then add rectangles behind the free-form shapes. I like my grids to curve, to give it a more flowing feeling! You can see this clearly in Illustration 2. Which pattern I choose for each shape depends on the amount of black it contains. If each square is filled with lots of lines, then it creates a pattern with high density. (Hence, the more black.) If there is lots of white in the pattern, then it is of low density. It is best to alternate between these two when you are working with overlapping shapes. If both are of the same density, then the eye sees confusion and misses the effect you are trying to create.

This was a real challenge with the realistic landscape in ILLUSTRATION 1. I needed to find an open pattern for the grass that complemented both the density of the pattern on the boat and the dense pattern of the water. I really had to make sure that the lines in the water were close together to achieve the contrast I wanted.

Once all the pencil lines are on the drawing, I can stand back and see if the density effect is working. This is the final chance I have to change the choices I have made; then I am ready to go over the lines with a fine-line marker.

Like a zentangle, my approach requires you to focus on each stroke and not the pattern. This allows you to relax and forces the mind away from any conflicts you are feeling, hence the word "zen" in my coined term "zen drawings." In other words, slow down! You can even turn the paper if this helps you make each stroke flow easier. When you come to an intersection of two lines, make sure they "just touch." This is where my white, fine-line marker comes in. I use it as my eraser.

The other thing I stress to my students is, don't strangle the pen! Stop and shake your fingers if you feel yourself tensing up! If I am at home and not listening to television, I will put on some instrumental music to help me stay relaxed. Over time, and the better you know each pattern, relaxation will become easier. The medical world calls this relaxed focus "mindfulness." You are forced to focus on only what your pen is doing.

Take some time to study these drawings and take the time to practice before you move on to adding color because the world of black and white and abstractions is intriguing and can help you take your interest in doodling into the realm of gallery art.

## Adding Color to the Borders

My main focus in my patterns is the appreciation for the positive and negative space and the play of contrast between overlapping forms. When you add color, the eye is distracted more easily to another area, depending on your choice of colors. Therefore, I usually use color only as an accent in my abstracts. I started with metallic markers in silver and gold. My fear has always been that I didn't want my drawing to look like coloring book pages, but with encouragement from friends, I have used other colors to enhance my work.

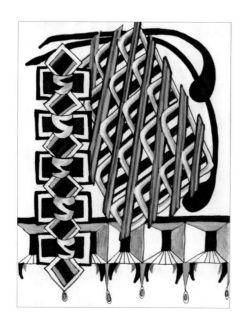

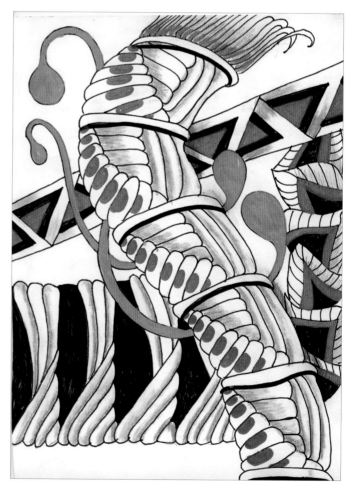

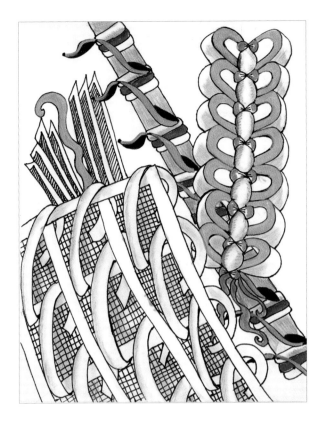

I have even moved into coloring the entire work. I especially like working with Derwent® watercolor pencils. The pigment is more intense than the more inexpensive pencils, though you do start as if you are coloring a drawing with coloring pencils using a family of colors as shading. As an example, let's consider the red family. The dark shadow would be red plus blue, the medium would be pure red, and the light would be orange. After I have colored in my shape with these colors, I take a damp brush and blend the colors together just as I did with the blending stump to the pencil smudge.

I also have used the markers that come with a blending marker that allow you to blend one color easily into another. What coloring technique you use is really a wide-open opportunity for you to explore. Whatever you are comfortable with start there, then try something new. Once you have learned these patterns, you have a structure to work within. The media is what will keep it interesting. I discovered that when I tried to take my pattern ideas to the medium of gourds, I really have enjoyed this style of drawing and have taken it even further. If you would like to see more, then please visit my Zen Drawing Gallery online at www. zendrawinggallery.com.

# Chapter 4:
## Exploring the World of Gourd Art

Patches are a good place to learn about new products.

There so many new people coming to this art form that I am pleased to offer my experience and suggestions on getting started. We "gourders" are famous for telling others, "Anything you can do to wood, you can do to a gourd and it's cheaper!" Most people think birdhouses when they think of what to do with gourds, but, really, this object has so much potential that you will be amazed. You can paint it, dye it, carve it, or wood-burn it. You can also cut the top off and use the gourd as a vessel or find a tall gourd to make a spirit doll or a small one to make a Christmas tree ornament.

I discovered gourd art after retiring from art education. I was in search of a new art media to learn. I mentioned this to an art teacher friend and she showed up on my doorstep, gourd in hand, with a terrible paint job done by a fifth grader who had left it in the art room. Initially, it didn't inspire me. Weeks later, it fell off the shelf and cracked. I hit it with a hammer to break it up

for the trash, but then I noticed the pieces were weightless and they reminded me of clay pot shards. Suddenly, the inspiration hit me with the idea of turning them into jewelry! What a hit that was! Four years later, I am now selling my gourd jewelry at festivals and art fairs.

You don't have to venture into this art media alone. There is a national organization and state organizations you can join. They sponsor gourd competitions for local groups they call "patches," and most states have them. Here, in Phoenix, most of the groups are made up of "baby boomers" and retirees like me who love the idea of working with easy power tools to make art objects to give to friends and family. The patches meet once a month to share ideas, learn from monthly demonstrations, and "show and tell" about their latest gourd creations. When you join a group, you can ask questions, get advice about tools and techniques, and share experiences, as well as make new friends.

Arizona has a longer growing season for gourds.

The gourds are picked green and then they dry in the hot Arizona sun.

The farm sells over 250,000 gourds a year.

## Buying and Cleaning Gourds

If you have a big enough space, sunlight, and lots of water, you can grow your own gourds. It is not easy, though, and I don't have the water budget here in Phoenix. Luckily for me, there is a great farm nearby in Casa Grande, Arizona, that provides many artists with gourds perfect for art-making. The Wuertz Farm (www.wuertzfarm.com) even sells and sends gourds overseas. They grow over 300,000 gourds a year! They are picked green and then they have to dry in the hot Arizona sun until they mold. They come in all sizes and shapes and you buy them according to the diameter of the gourd.

There is food, entertainment and places to rest before exploring more vendors with gourd art ready for collecting.

Gourds are separated by shape and size for easy selection.

I soak as many as I can and usually spend 3-4 hours cleaning.

The best way to purchase them is at the Wuertz Gourd Festival. This event is the largest gourd festival in the United States, with over a hundred vendors, many classes by expert gourd artists, and one of the most challenging gourd competitions endorsed by the American Gourd Association and sponsored by the Arizona Gourd Society. The three-day event in February attracts over 10,000 gourd artists, collectors, and admirers every year. You can hand-pick your gourds on site and carry them home in the car. If you do get to choose your own, be sure to check that the gourd sits flat on the ground! Many will not, and then you may need to create legs for it or find a stand. This was my worse beginner's mistake, plus I had chosen gourds with pretty mold patterns that I later learned I had to scrape off. If it is flaking off as it sits there, it is a good thing!

Tools can be bought online or at festivals.

Another great location for buying gourds is Welburn Farm in California. They also ship boxes of gourds, and will even ship them cleaned and cut. You can check them out at www.welburngourdfarm.com. Other states also sell gourds at their state gourd festivals, or perhaps you can find a farmer in your area that grows them.

Gourds are available in many sizes and have been used by every culture on this planet. Some still grow wild, while others are grown on farms and in backyards. It is not easy and takes lots of space and water, so I just drive to the farm and choose my favorites from the outdoor bins.

All dried gourds are covered with a waxy surface that has to be removed. Some people are allergic to the spores, so wearing a mask is a great safety tip for everyone. I start by filling a big plastic container with water and dish soap and then I submerge the gourds for about an hour to help loosen the waxy coating. Another great idea is to put them in a heavy plastic garbage bag with soap and water and let it sit in the sun for several hours. Do not leave them in water overnight! They will crack! There is a way to fill the crack with glue, but avoid the problem if you can.

Next, gather some tools to help you clean off the mold and be sure to put on your mask. I start with a kitchen scouring pad to take off the loose particles and then move to the special tools made for this task. I wear an apron and place a towel under the gourd. This keeps me dry and helps keep the gourd on my lap. My favorite tool is this scraper, which comes as a set of two from The Caning Shop. Other tools you might use include a paring knife and a sanding sponge.

I like doing this outside wearing a mask. All of the mold has to be removed with whatever tool works best.

Scrapers come in several different sizes.

Once the gourd is clean and dry, you can break it into shards or consider cutting the top off to create a vessel. I recommend a special gourd saw. Most of my gourd tools and supplies I purchase online. My favorite vendor for tools is The Caning Shop (www.caning.com); owner Jim Widess researches every item he sells. His criteria for his selection of tools includes: superior customer support, the lasting quality of the product, and its ease and comfort in use. He even answers the phone! He has replaced broken tools with no questions asked. Gourd festivals are a great place to check out tools and supplies. Vendors demonstrate their wares and are eager to answer your questions.

Once the gourd is clean, I then use my gourd sander and clean away the small white spots and any remaining wax areas. If I have planned to leave the gourd its natural color, I will sand it with a finer grain until it shines! Next, I cut off the top. I draw a line where I want to cut into the gourd. I use a sharp knife to puncture a short line into the gourd to create an entry point for the saw blade and then, with the gourd saw, I slowly cut the gourd. With that, the next cleaning process is suddenly revealed.

This is the gourd saw I purchased from The Caning Shop.

The sander includes replaceable discs.

Sometimes it is dry enough to flake off, other times you need to scrape hard.

Sometimes I sprinkle glitter on the big seeds and turn them into earrings!

You never know what you have until you cut the top off!

## Cleaning the Inside of the Gourd

Be sure your mask is still on because this is the nasty part for some people. You will need to gather you're inside cleaning tools to help you completely clean out the inside. I use the same scraping tool I used on the outside. Scrape out the seeds and the white spongy surface.

You might want to keep the seeds and use them as embellishments, or make earrings, or plant them. If they are meaty on the inside, they will grow! My patch saves them and sells them at the festival.

Here is where I want to point out a very interesting detail. Not all gourds are the same thickness. If you are going to carve a gourd, then a thicker one is a better choice. After holding several of the same size, you will begin to notice that some are heavier than others. Also keep in mind that thicker gourds are harder to cut, but really thin gourds crack easily.

The last step is to sand the inside so it is smooth. Use whatever tool you can find. I always start out with course sandpaper and an old spoon. Sandpaper sponges are also useful on the rim. Many gourd artists use the metal ball sanders that are attached to a drill. They come with handles in different lengths. Most gourd suppliers carry them. Make sure the bottom of the inside is flat and the pointed ridge in the center is gone. Wipe away the dust inside with a damp paper towel before painting.

My final step is

Competition gourds really need to be clean. They check closely!

to pour black acrylic paint into the interior and brush it all over the inside surface. Dark colors work best. Some artists use spray-paint for this part, but I always seem to get it on the outside by mistake. Some artists suggest covering the rim with masking tape before spraying.

Now you are done and ready for the art part! The cleaning process is often done as a "patch cleaning party," which includes a potluck and lots of stories of worst cleaning experiences. The cleaning process is the part that is the least fun! For more tool ideas, join a patch and ask questions.

# Wood-burning on Gourds

Pyrography is a Greek word that means "writing with fire." It's a good thing they started with wood because if they had started wood-burning on gourds, the whole art form may have died out! It's not easy "writing with fire" on a curved surface that is not smooth and may be waxy in spots! To say the least, it takes patience and the right tools. Yet it can be relaxing and very rewarding.

The most important factor for gourd artists is control. Some of us are light-handed while some of us, like me, are heavy-handed. Look at wire-nib burners with variable temperature controls. The writing nib is heated by an electrical current passing directly through it. Some models have interchangeable nibs to allow for different effects. There are several brands to check out: Colwood (www.woodburning.com); Razertip® (www.sawdustconnection.com); and Sabre. (From the latter, I own the Detail Master™, which can deliver up to 100 watts of power. More information about this toolcan be found at www.detailmasteronline.com/systems.html.).

Some artists like the permanent tips while others like the replaceable pen tips. These tools are expensive. You can plan on spending around $200 for a system and around $30 for a handle plus tips — but the system will last a lifetime. This is where a "patch" can be useful. Visit one first and ask other gourd artists which burners they use and why? Maybe they will even let you try

theirs before you buy it. I would also recommend you purchase two other items: a small table fan to blow the smoke away from your eyes and an apron to keep the small ashes from burning tiny holes in your clothes. Others also suggest wearing a paper mask. Always turn the burner off when it is not in use. Most of all, be patient with yourself and begin with shards, not gourds. However, if you really want to master the wood-burner before you even start on gourds, read ahead and learn how to wood-burn on soft wood first. All of my borders started on gourd shards long before I started putting them onto prepared gourds. It is much easier to throw a shard away than a gourd that took an hour to clean!

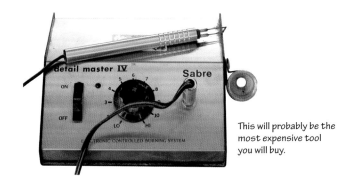

This will probably be the most expensive tool you will buy.

These are easy to show off and collect for later reference.

I like how the ruler bends and I can clearly see the gourd underneath.

Always clean and lightly sand the shard after wood-burning to make the color application easier.

## Practice on a Shard

Gourd artists often buy the cracked gourds to use for practice. I usually clean the gourd first. I then wrap it in a towel and hit it several times with a hammer, breaking the gourd into large pieces. I then clean the back and sand off the corners. Now, you can wood-burn fearlessly!

Using shards is also a great way to try out different color schemes before you go to your gourd. My patch turns them into refrigerator magnets that we sell at the gourd festivals, which helps us pay for demonstration instructors — so don't throw the good ones away!

Once I have decided on a pattern, I begin by using the ruler to create the grid on the shard lightly in pencil and then I wood-burn the pattern row by row, doing the lines all going to the right. Next, I turn the shard around to get the other lines so I can keep burning with a right-hand motion. Place the gourd securely in front of you and don't be afraid to turn it as you work on it. Find the most comfortable position for your hand holding the burner. When I am finished, I use a paper towel and a small spray bottle with 90% isopropyl/rubbing alcohol. This cleans away the pencil marks and ash marks of the wood-burner. I then give it a light sanding with very fine sandpaper. It is ready for a color medium.

This gourd is 10" in diameter and 7" high.

The back of the gourd. I thought this straight lined pattern would look interesting hanging from this wavy edge.

## Shutter Wing Gourd

Once the gourd is cleaned and painted on the inside, you are ready to draw your pattern on the outside. You will need to bring out your soft drawing pencil and eraser, the clear plastic ruler, and, perhaps, your grid index paper. When you are finished with the burning, remember to use your small spray bottle of 90% rubbing alcohol and a soft cloth or paper towel to clean your gourd before you apply the paint. I like to use a spray varnish two days after the gourd is finished.

I used the ruler to create a line 3/4" from the top and another line at the bottom of the design. I then sketched in the grid and the pattern, adjusting as I go because of the curved surface.

I determined that the gourd will have a front with a center embellishment, so I have outlined the shape of the copper circle. Next, I clean up the lines with the curved ruler, making them straighter.

This is where I decided the squiggly lines were too powerful, so I turned them into arrows. Artists can change things as they proceed. Just go with what looks best.

Once I see that the lines are straight and clear, I can begin to wood burn the pattern. I started with the top edge, and then I burned all the vertical lines down from that edge.

Next, I turn the gourd upside down and burned the diagonal lines. I followed the same process on the interior lines. Next, I did the arrows.

When the burning was completed, I lightly sanded the area and cleaned the surface. Next, I painted the background, to help me visualize the effect of the color scheme I wanted use.

## Tiger Shell Gourd

I used two patterns on this gourd: Triline on the top and Tiger Shell along the middle. I want to share two new products with you that are very useful for beginners. A good friend of mine, Miriam Joy (www.miriamjoy.com), came up with these rubber circle guides that are available in many different sizes — and she even has them in squares! Also, I purchased the narrow (1/4") masking tape online at Welburn Gourd Farm (www.welburngourdfarm.com).

The coloring media and techniques are endless, and there are many books and classes at gourd festivals that you can take advantage of once you feel confident with your drawing and wood burning skills. On this gourd, I used gourd dyes, acrylic paints, and a copper acrylic paint, which I have a passion for! Just try everything! After I photograph it, I give it two coats of spray varnish, but don't get too close — or the varnish will drip! Let it dry overnight between coats.

This gourd is 9" tall and 6" in diameter.

This is an easy way to draw a double edge line around a gourd.

To secure them to the gourd, I used a masking tape that comes in a 1/4" roll.

I used the tape to create the borders that separate the two patterns.

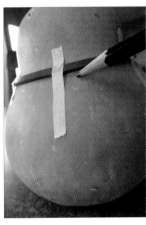

I just draw on either side of the tape

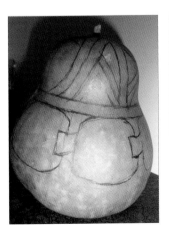

I created my grids and drew my pattern in heavy pencil.

I wood-burned the border pattern and cleaned and sanded the design.

Instead of using paint on this gourd, I applied an ink dye.

You can use a sponge for the large area and one of these small tip applicators for outlining around your border. Welburn Gourd Farm carries all these products and more.

# Chapter 5: Carving the Border Patterns

## Using Soft Wood

I have been wood burning and carving wood for several years now. I display my work at woodworking shows and give classes at woodworking stores in the Valley of the Sun area. I can see many possibilities with these patterns in my own work and look forward to sharing them with my carving students. Bettie is opening the doors for many of us with her creative patterns and I can't wait to build from many of her designs. I call it "stepping stones to creativity," so with that said, grab your pencil and put your thinking cap on and let's go. I am going talk about wood selection, sand paper, wood burning tips, carving gouges, and a few finishes I like to use.

The projects featured here are wood-burned and/or wood-carved. The size of the pattern dictates what size carving knife and gouges you should use. As you can see, I used a variation of different gouges and detail knives. I used a small or larger skew, writer, and shader based on size of pattern and design.

### Wood Selection

Woods that I prefer carving on are bass wood, butternut, tupelo, mahogany, pine, and poplar. Remember that when wood burning and/or sanding, be sure you have good ventilation. When selecting your wood, be sure to avoid knots and wood that has started warping.

### Sanding Notes

Softer woods respond very well with 220-320 grit. Based on how hard the wood and how rough of a cut available, you may have to start at 150-180 grit. Use a tack cloth after sanding or brushing your project before you apply the paint, stain, or top coat. You will need to remove all the saw dust and especially any residual grit from sandpaper. The grit from the sandpaper will definitely dull the carving tools.

Bettie encourages everyone to hand-draw the patterns on to a project media, which is the best way; not only is it fastest, but it also develops self-growth in pattern designing. Once the wood is sanded and the pattern is drawn on the wood, it is time to heat up the wood burning tool!

### Wood-burning tips

I use only three or four different wood-burning tips on most of my projects. My favorite is a skew tip; then a writer and shaders. The size of your project will dictate the size of skew width and shaders depending on how much rounding, squared off edges, or sharp angles you will be facing during the designing process. The writer tip is handy when you do not want a deep burn and it is a great way to sign your project.

Practice with the tips before you start. You can also try outlining, shading, and stippling with the tips. Explore each tip to see what it can do. After burning, I use a wire brush or even a toothbrush (soft-mild to firm) to get rid of charred wood specks. Take care of your tips by cleaning with a leather strop with honing compound. Tips work best when they are clean and sharp!

Helvie detail knife.

V parting tool

### Carving the details

If you are inclined, you can try my favorite skill: carving wood. In every style of carving, you use a detail knife. If you are working with softer woods, the flex cut brand will work very well. When working with harder wood, do yourself a favor and use a forged blade detail knife, i.e. Helvie knives. I use for both soft and harder woods. They hold an edge nicely and that makes carving a real pleasure.

Gouge sizes vary based on sweep and width of tool. The Swiss brand has two measurements listed on their tools: the first one represents the sweep of the tool; the second number is the width of the tool. The Swiss tools are measured in metric, so always remember that a flat chisel will be the first number (#1) — the higher the number, the more the sweep or curvature of the tool. The V, or parting tool, sizes vary based on angle degree.

# Carving the Springfly Pattern

Let's get started with the Springfly pattern. By using one of Bettie's pattern ideas with some of my own ideas, I sketched the pattern onto a piece of basswood. The first thing you will do with the pattern is to stop cut. Take your detail knife and cut on top of the outline of the pattern. This prevents unwanted chipping and helps your outlines to look clean. It also helps you control your cuts with a knife or when using a gouge. Once the stop cut is finished, you can get started carving.

After creating stop cuts, I make an angle cut on the right side of the stop cut. The different degree of angle cut determines how deep you want your carving around the pattern design. Notice that I shaded areas on the pattern, so I know there will be areas deeper than others to create the different level and pattern definition.

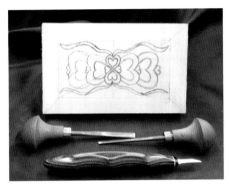
This pattern is drawn on the wood with a soft lead pencil.

I am using the cutting tool and inserting it into the pencil line.

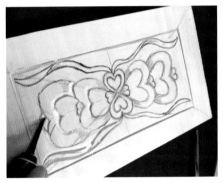
I hold my knife at a 45- or 65-degree angle.

To create a radius or round off, simply turn the gouge over and gently carve the edge off.

After a little sanding, this project is ready for stain. I will use gel stain since they are very easy to use.

The finished project.

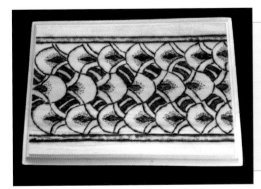

I just love this pattern. By using Bettie's pattern idea, I added stipling to the project so it enhances the vision of lilies. When I added the bold lines, I think it gave it the effect of being bumble bees. I now call this design mine, since I made modifications. I call it "Lilly Patch."
**Endless bloom wood-burned on soft wood.**

# Adding Stains and a Finish

Adding stain to your piece can add depth and texture, bringing out nuances in the carving that would not be as visible without the stain. If you are using a water-based stain, apply multiple coats with a synthetic type of pad vs. steel wool. Steel and water don't mix well. If you are buffing between coats with steel wool, you can leave steel particles in the wood, but rust will result after water exposure. There are four different types of synthetic pads to use: Green (very coarse and most aggressive), Maroon (coarse), Gray (medium), and White (finest). Buy and use them all.

## Acrylics on Wood Surfaces

You can also choose to use acrylic paints on the wood surface. I use Jo Sonja's acrylic paints and brushes on my woodcarving projects. Since I put a lot time and love into my projects, I want them to have the ultimate paint and finish.

You can also add different top coats to your finished wood piece. You should consider protecting the wood from the elements with a shellac or lacquer finish. Poly-acrylic lacquer are non-yellowing top coats. Coating the surface with shellac, tung oil, urethane, and linseed oil will add a hint of amber to your project.

It's great if you want your project to have an aged or warming appearance.

If you are a woodworker, the opportunities are endless with Bettie's helpful designs and hints. These patterns offer you the opportunity to expand your own creativity and skills. Consider embellishing trinket boxes, bowls, frames, and plaques. You could also add these patterns to lazy susans, furniture, cabinetry, and more. Have fun making your unique projects with these helpful hints.

# Conclusion

To carve on a gourd, you will need a rotary tool kit or most probably a Dremel® tool. I highly recommend you also buy the flex shaft attachment. It makes the entire carving process so much easier!

There are three basic types of attachment shapes you will need. Most gourd artists use high-speed steel burs. You will need a wheel for cutting through the gourd or on the surface; a ball for general fast removal of the skin; and a cylinder or an inverted cone. Once you have decided to take carving seriously, you can move up to the Carbide burs, which are more expensive but outlive the steel ones. Just remember to use them on low speed on your Dremel. Stay away from the diamond burs because they do not work well on the gourd skin. I like the dovetail shape for basketry and ripples. When I work in tight, close areas, I use a taper shape that I also use for flattening background areas.

I use the 1" wheel to drag across the surface of the gourd to take the skin off in large areas and then the 1/4" wheel to skin the gourd close to my wood burning. There are so many attachments that it is oftentimes confusing. That's why I recommend you take a class or a demonstration from someone who has established they're own technique. They will always have a list of attachments they prefer. The carving expert in my area is Bonnie Gibson and she has a website (http://arizonagourds.homestead.com/CarvingBurs.html) where she sells and explains the advantages of all the tips she uses when carving. She only sells what she uses and offers in her award-winning gourd classes. I also suggest you check out another Arizona gourd carver, Phyllis Sickles (http://www.gourdvisions.com/Index.html); her work is amazing and inspiring. She also has great photo directions of her technique, which has really helped me as I have just begun to work in this area.

Whether you carve on wood or gourds, this can be a very exciting hobby with lots of groups around to help you. At the last woodcarving show I attended, I expected to see most of the women members' wood burning, but I was very excited when I saw Janet and several other women with prize-winning carvings. I would think that the small hand of a woman could carve small items better, but everyone there assured me that it really just takes patience and practice and the men love having all the women around to tease…so this is another group of artists you need to check out.

Enjoy the patterns and by all means extend your horizons into the world of gourds and wood. I hope I have inspired you to reach out beyond your current comfort zone to try your hand at these doodles in several media until you make them your own. And don't forget to show me your results! You can find my addresses and those of other artists mentioned in this book on the Acknowledgments page. GO HAVE FUN!

# Acknowledgments

I would like to thank the many friends I have encountered in the gourd world here in Arizona. Every month I attend two "patches": the Southwest Gourd Association in Phoenix and the New River Patch in New River, Arizona. Members in each patch have taught me so much about gourds, small power tools, and the desert. With their encouragement, I began this book and welcomed their willingness to share their work with you. Many of the examples of gourd art are from them.

I especially want to thank Janet Bolyard for her expert advice on tools and tips for woodburning and woodcarving on wood. I often show my gourd jewelry at woodworking shows and was thrilled to meet such a talented artist willing to help a novice wood-burner. Friends are everywhere in the art world. In fact, they are just a question away, so I encourage you to reach out to a group or a class offered at an art show. All these artists have enriched my life.

I also want to thank the most important man in my life, Ray, for his endless encouragement.

Here are the artists that made items that illustrate this book. I hope you will visit their websites and consider collecting some of their artwork. For those without websites, you can e-mail me for their address at bettie.lake@gmail.com.

Gretchen Boyer

Bev Felber

Prill Neagles

Ana Mayse

Janet Bolyard
Email: janetleecarving@yahoo.com

Karen Friend
Soaring Spirit Studio
www.soaringspiritstudio.com

Beatriz Castro
My Silk Way
www.mysilkway.com

Dar Saucedo
Gourdgeous by Design
www.gourdgeousbydesign.com

Danielle Selby
Gourd Art By Danielle
www.gourdartbydanielle.com

Hellenne Vermillion
Vermillion Silk Artist
www.vermillionsilkartist.com

Jane Boggs
Jane Boggs Fine Art
www.janeboggsgourdart.com

Bettie Lake
Gourd Blossom Jewelry
www.gourdblossomjewelry.com
Zen Drawings
www.zendrawinggallery.com

## VENDORS

Wuertz Farm
www.wuertzfarm.com

Welburn Gourd Farm
www.welburngourdfarm.com

Arizona's Gourd Competition and Festival
www.arizonagourdsociety.org

The Caning Shop
www.caning.com

Bonnie Gibson
http://arizonagourds.homestead.com

Miriam Joy
www.miriamjoy.com

American Gourd Society
www.americangourdsociety.org